Born to be
Worthless

The Hidden Power
of
Low Self-Esteem

by Dr. Kevin Solomons
MD, FRCPC

ISBN: 148114071X
ISBN-13: 9781481140713

Library of Congress Control Number: 2012923688
Createspace Independent Publishing Platform
North Charleston, South Carolina

"There is nothing either good or bad,
but thinking makes it so....
I could be bounded in a nutshell,
and count myself a king of infinite space."

— *William Shakespeare, Hamlet*

ACKNOWLEDGEMENTS

We humans define ourselves by our unique ability to learn. Instead of Homo Sapiens, we might have as easily classified ourselves as Homo Studens. We learn both intentionally and inadvertently, when we expect to and when we least expect to. This is how it has been and still is for me. I am profoundly grateful to all the people I have and continue to learn from. This includes all my teachers, instructors and mentors over the years. I am especially indebted to the authors who have more directly informed my understanding of the matters addressed in this book. They include Jean Piaget, the founder of cognitive development, Richard Dawkins, author of the thought provoking and enlightening book The Selfish Gene, John Bowlby, doyen of our understanding of attachment, separation and loss, Viktor Frankl's existential and humanistic treasures, Aaron Beck and David Burns, outstanding proponents of cognitive behavior therapy, and Dr. Gail Saltz's illuminating insights in her book Becoming Real. Where would we be without all these inspired and inspiring thought leaders?

Tamara Letkeman and Nadine Pedersen of Black Swan Services were invaluable in getting this manuscript into shape, and without James Basnett of Slate West I could not have established my website and online presence. I am particularly thankful to the Project Team 5 at CreateSpace for their courteous and efficient help in bringing this manuscript to life and for demystifying the hitherto arcane process of publishing. My special thanks go to Rachel Rothbart for frequently and so generously proofing and copy editing the manuscript.

I am indebted to all the patients I have been privileged to work with, from whom I have learned so much and by whom I have been provoked to learn even more. The input from colleagues and friends has been and remains inestimable. My family has been and remains an enduring source of stimulation, insight and not always invited but nonetheless invaluable feedback.

Without my wife Deborah's original suggestion to commit the core ideas of this work to paper, together with her constant encouragement, support, suggestions and eagle-eyed critiques, this book would not have come into being.

I hope that in some small way, this work pays back even an iota of my huge debt to everyone who has informed and enriched my life.

DEDICATION

For Deborah

CONTENTS

ZOSSEL xi

INTRODUCTION xiii

PART ONE: BECOMING INFORMED: WHAT YOU NEED TO KNOW TO BE WORTHWHILE

CHAPTER 1
MY PATH TO DISCOVERY 3

CHAPTER 2
THE ORIGINS OF SELF-ESTEEM 21

CHAPTER 3
THE CHANGING NATURE OF NEED 37

CHAPTER 4
NARCISSISM AND COGNITIVE DEVELOPMENT 49

CHAPTER 5
LOW SELF-ESTEEM AND THE IMPERATIVE TO PLEASE 65

CHAPTER 6
FROM PLEASING TO PERSONALITY: CREATING YOUR
PERSONALITY 75

CHAPTER 7
COERCION: THE ALTERNATIVE TO PLEASING 89

CHAPTER 8
WHEN PLEASING FAILS 101

CHAPTER 9
STRESS AND THE ONSET OF SYMPTOMS 117

CHAPTER 10
THE HIGH VALUE OF LOW SELF-ESTEEM 125

PART TWO: PUTTING WHAT YOU'VE LEARNED INTO PRACTICE

CHAPTER 11
TRANSCENDING LOW SELF-ESTEEM 139

CHAPTER 12
INFORMED DECISION MAKING 147

CHAPTER 13
THE IMPLICATIONS OF CHOOSING HEALTHY SELF-ESTEEM...... 161

CHAPTER 14
PRACTICE... 175

CHAPTER 15
CHANNELING JENNY 185

CHAPTER 16
IN A NUTSHELL 187

ZOSSEL

My friend Hillel tells the charming story of a man called Zossel who dies and goes to heaven. Upon arrival at the outer gates, Zossel meets the Almighty and pleads his case for entry into paradise. He chronicles the myriad ways in which he honored the commandments, prayed regularly as prescribed, gave generously to the needy, honored his parents, was kind to all, never missed a religious service, and studied with the great teachers of the day. He was a model citizen, congregant, student, husband, and father, and a faithful servant of the Lord. When he finished his submission, the Holy One was quiet, looked him closely, and said, "Yes, yes, you were surely a good man, but were you Zossel?"

INTRODUCTION

As we enter the second decade of the new millennium, studies are revealing that the days of people repeating self-empowerment expressions to boost their self-esteem are over. Not only this, but that mantras of self-affirmation can actually harm, rather than help, people who suffer from low self-esteem.[1] The idea of "I'm good enough, I'm smart enough, and doggone it, people like me!" just won't cut it anymore. The fact that you have picked up this book attests to the notion that it's likely not cutting it with you anymore, either.

In *Born To Be Worthless: The Hidden Power Of Low Self-Esteem*, I introduce a new and dramatically different approach to overcoming low self-esteem. I believe that it is crucial to understand the origins of our low self-esteem before being able to transcend it. I believe that self-esteem develops and emerges during early childhood, before we can remember. It is my contention that our first and enduring understanding of our self-worth is that we are expendable, that we are not worthwhile, and that we need to induce others to treat us as though we were worthwhile in order to feel worthwhile. I argue that we do not know how to make ourselves feel worthwhile on our own and

---

1 J. Wood, W. Elaine Perunovic, and J. Lee,, "Positive Self-Statements: Power for Some, Peril for Others," Psychological Science 20 (7): 860-66, doi:10.1111/j.1467-9280.2009.02370.x

that unless we specifically learn how to value ourselves, we go to our graves depending on others for a sense of positive self-worth.

I will explain why this dependency on others for self-worth comes about and has currency, even though it seems so limiting. I will make a case for changing the arrangement of relying on others for self-worth and learning to rely on yourself instead, and show how this change is possible and how to accomplish it.

To replace others and becoming your own source of self-worth you need to make an informed decision to become the source of your worth, and then put this decision into action to make it true for you.

The information needed for this decision incorporates an understanding of the origins of your self-esteem, so that you can appreciate the flawed basis on which you formed your views of your self-worth, or lack thereof. It involves adopting a realistic understanding and appreciation of the world and the nature of reality, in contrast to the distorted view you acquired in early childhood. This information is vital for the next step, which is making a very specific decision about whether and on what terms your life is worth having.

Having made an informed decision to be worthwhile, in other words, to be your own source of worth, you then have to put this decision into practice decided. Only through practicing being worthwhile can you become worthwhile.

This process of giving life to your decision is essentially one of changing an old habit, in this case, the thought habit of having your worth determined by others, and replacing it with the new thought of being the one to determine your own worth. There are many different approaches to changing habits, and I propose a simple three-step approach that I refer to as the three Rs of emotional literacy: recognize, remember, and rehearse.

"Recognize" refers to recognizing your old, patterned ways of making sense of and responding to situations, "Remember" means remembering the new and different way you have decided to be, and "Rehearse" refers to trying out different ways of behaving as someone who is responsible for your self-worth rather than as someone whose worth is determined by others.

It's worth mentioning at the outset that all the information and all the steps required to achieve this, to become the source of your own worth, are readily within the grasp of everybody. Some of the concepts are a little complex and require attention and effort to master; effort is definitely required to practice being the person you decide to be, since changing old habits is never easy, but always possible. There are no obstacles to achieving healthy self-esteem other than a lack of interest and commitment.

This book contains the information and the steps necessary to enable you to acquire healthy and positive self-esteem. Armed with the information, you will soon be ready and able to become your own source of healthy self-worth.

PART ONE:

BECOMING INFORMED:WHAT YOU NEED TO KNOW TO BE WORTHWHILE

CHAPTER 1

MY PATH TO DISCOVERY

"Physician, heal thyself."

— *Luke 4:23*

I began my psychiatry training twenty-five years ago, at the tail end of the psychoanalytic era and at the beginning of the brain chemical (neurotransmitter and psychopharmacological) era. I was exposed to both of these very different approaches to the study of the mind. I was intrigued by the exoticism and eroticism of psychoanalysis, the beautiful writing of Freud and many of his followers, and a prurient interest in their cliquey personal lives and cutthroat politics. I was equally inspired by the boldness of the new scientific frontiersmen, the breed of neuroscientists who were mapping neurotransmitter pathways and relating brain chemicals to our moods and thoughts and behaviors.

Neurotransmitter research was inextricably linked with psycho-pharmacology (or mind drugs) to treat a raft of psychiatric ailments. Suddenly we had weapons to treat illnesses in whose presence we were previously powerless. The antidepressants and antipsychotic medications we prescribed were potent, often highly effective, and accompanied by strong side effects. (We used to say that drugs with no side effects had no front effects.) Only the sickest and most desperate of patients would willingly agree to take them.

The early victories of the brain chemical movement soon led to the displacement of psychoanalysis as a framework for understanding and treating depressed and anxious people. The demise of psycho-analysis passed mostly unmourned in the modern schools of psychiatry, and psychopharmacologists and neuroscientists replaced psycho-analysts as faculty in psychiatry programs and as leaders in the field. Psychoanalysis was regarded as a quaint and faintly embarrassing reminder of an ineffectual, inglorious and somewhat self-indulgent past.

Even though psychoanalysis lost ground, psychology itself could not be dismissed, and watered-down versions of psychoanalysis called psychotherapy emerged in a profusion of different styles. In time, some psychotherapists jumped on the bandwagon of evidence-based practice, the mark of credibility of the new scientific, or biological, era. Psychotherapy outcome studies were published that demonstrated the merits of these new forms of psychological treatments and they took their place alongside the now more popular pharma-cological treatments of psychiatric and psychological conditions.

There were likely many pressures moving psychotherapy in this direction of evidence-based practice, including the requirements of third-party payers such as the medical insurance industry, which needed to justify the expense of psychotherapy by showing that it had therapeutic benefits. Therapies that could be distilled into a manual and especially those that lent themselves to group therapy gained favor, none more so than cognitive behavior therapy (CBT), which has since become the mainstay of psychological treatment for depression, anxiety and related disorders. Psychology can now be had in a bottle, so to speak.

From my vantage point as a psychiatrist working in a tertiary mood disorders clinic at the University of British Columbia, I have come to appreciate the shortcomings of both the psychopharmacologic and psychotherapeutic approaches. People who respond well and early to either medications and/or psychotherapy generally do not attend the mood disorder clinic, so the people who do come have usually not responded to standard treatments. Frequently we see people who have been treated with a plethora of different antidepressants and other psychiatric medications in a variety of combinations. Many of these people have also been treated with psychotherapy or counseling of some form, usually CBT.

SELF-ESTEEM: CAUSE OR EFFECT OF DEPRESSION?

In all my years of working with depressed and anxious people, it has become glaringly obvious that very few, or more likely none, had healthy self-esteem. In fact, just about everybody I saw had terrible self-esteem. In one way or another, they all regarded themselves as worthless failures. The Diagnostic and Statistical Manual of the American Psychiatric Association lists "feelings of worthlessness" as one of the cardinal symptoms for the diagnosis of a major depression. It is assumed that feelings of worthlessness, like the other diagnostic symptoms, are not present when the person is not depressed and are therefore symptomatic of an altered state, the state of depression. In the same vein, in successfully treating the depression, the depressive symptoms, including feelings of worthlessness, disappear and the hypothetical pre-depression state of positive self-esteem returns.

But as I listened to my patients, it became increasingly clear to me that low self-esteem was not merely a symptom of depression, but rather a longstanding attitude they had toward themselves, present long before the depression surfaced. In other words, the depression amplified a preexisting attitude rather than creating it from scratch. Furthermore, when the symptoms of depression (low mood, poor sleep, fatigue, low energy, joylessness, loss of interest, social withdrawal and so on) made it difficult or impossible for people to do the things that normally made them feel worthwhile, they were left feeling guilty, futile and worthless for underfunctioning. This typically worsened the experience of depression. Feeling worthless not only made people feel depressed in the first place, in their depressed state it made them feel even more depressed and became a vicious cycle. I reached the conclusion that low self-esteem, far from being just a symptom, is instead an important *cause* of depression.

It also dawned on me that low self-esteem is not confined to people who had difficult and unloving childhoods. Instead, it seemed to affect everyone, including people who reported positive loving and supportive childhoods. I was struck by the reports of low self-worth from patients who came from a wide variety of family backgrounds and remembered childhoods—from families that were loving and nurturing to families that were cruel, neglectful, and abusive. Just as depression showed no regard for culture, class, gender, or family circumstances, self-esteem seemed to show the same disregard, and most astonishingly, *no* regard for family closeness or the degree of childhood nurturing. It seemed that low self-esteem was the outcome, regardless of whether a person was raised by nurturing loving parents or by indifferent, neglectful, or cruel ones.

This puzzled me, as my understanding of self-esteem was that positive self-esteem originates from the childhood experience of being loved and valued, while low self-esteem arose from the opposite. What I encountered in my practice seemed to contradict this understanding.

Furthermore, it seemed to me that we maintain positive self-esteem through the rest of our lives by being appreciated, valued and loved by others, and that we try to ensure that we remain loved and valued by pleasing others, often by achieving. There is a correlation between our achievements and our self-esteem, in that the better we do and the more we accomplish, the better we feel about ourselves.

But there is a contradiction. If positive self-esteem results from being well loved as a child, how does it come to be related to one's later achievements? Put another way, if positive self-esteem comes from good, loving experiences of childhood, why does it not last? Why do we need good, loving experiences (or their symbolic equivalents in the form of material success) to continue to feel worthwhile? And why, when we no longer feel loved and affirmed by others, do we feel worthless and miserable? What happens to the earlier experience of having been loved, and why does that not sustain us in times of disappointment and setback? And conversely, why can we not build lasting positive self-esteem from our later accomplishments, even if we had negative experiences and felt unloved earlier in our lives?

These were some of the questions that arose as I listened to person after person recount experiences of not responding to standard treatments of medications and therapy, and relating how much they hated themselves and felt like failures. Meanwhile, I sat there asking myself how these people could feel so bad about themselves when they had such warm and loving memories of their childhoods, had such loving parents/husbands/wives/children/friends, were so accomplished with apparently successful and fulfilling careers, were financially stable and led such seemingly interesting lives.

Born To Be Worthless: The Hidden Power Of Low Self-Esteem is about the answers to these questions. It is about the nature of self-esteem, its origins, and its impact on our lives. It is also, and most importantly, about what we can do to change our negative and failing self-esteem, especially when that low self-esteem expresses itself as misery, despair, anxiety and depression.

MY STORY

My thoughts and experience are not derived solely from the patients I've treated, but also from personal experience. I too have a story about low self-esteem and its impact on my life. Coming to an understanding of my experience has been an intricate part of the way I was able to develop the theories and methods described in this book. I will share some of the epiphanies of my journey with you.

I was raised in a small city in South Africa during the 1960s. My family was loving, educated, privileged, liberal, middle class and Jewish. My extended family all lived within a four-block radius of my home. The community was small, stable, tightknit and free of any major dramas—at least to my knowledge as a rather innocent and particularly naïve child. The community's progressive, liberal views, which in my case became more radical in favor of pro-democracy and anti-apartheid political change, made possible a comfortable coexistence with the horrors of apartheid. To an outsider, my life would have seemed stable and secure.

But in actuality my outward appearance of confidence and security was a marvelous illusion. Instead, I was emotionally very needy and constantly looking for reassurance and affirmation. I recall a close friend warning a potential girlfriend (who became my wife) to think carefully about getting involved with me, because I was so needy. At the time I didn't see myself that way; I was a driven overachiever who was bringing home the results (albeit without any understanding of what was driving me so hard to produce those results). As long as I was achieving, I felt good about myself.

But achieving was something I had to keep refreshing. Over time it became harder and harder to maintain a constant level of achievement. What's more, affirmation was difficult to come by. My professors didn't care about my grades; they didn't phone my parents to congratulate them on my performance. And besides, in the world of radical student politics, the focus was always on people who were the real and obvious victims—in this case the people who were victims of a grim and vicious political system. So in a world where attention was focused outward rather than inward—and appropriately so—affirmation became increasingly hard to come by.

With time I became increasingly aware of my insecurities and the methods I used to hide or counter them. I didn't like this image of myself as the needy person, so clearly articulated by my friend, but didn't really know how to deal with it other than by continuing to please others, mostly by achieving.

I have speculated a great deal about the roots of my insecurity and low self-esteem. As a psychiatrist, I have held a number of plausible theories at different times, depending often on which theorist I was reading or which therapist I was seeing. The theories inevitably involved my parents and something they had or hadn't done—things that I could still vividly and painfully recall. I crafted increasingly plausible accounts of their missteps that grew more sophisticated in tandem with my own professional experience and understanding. Eventually I arrived at a watertight version of their well-intentioned misdemeanors. It became my story, well packaged, fluent, plausible, and compelling. At least one of my sisters confirmed my version.

In my version, I am sure that I was sufficiently loved, appreciated, and attended to as a child. I was never abused and experienced no overwhelming trauma in my early life. My parents took excellent care of me. I was encouraged, supported, praised, and doted on.

In spite of this, I remember from an early age feeling that unless I did things to impress my parents, they would not notice me in the way that I felt I needed to be noticed. I determined that the way to get what I needed from them was to impress them. The way to do this was clear: do exceedingly well in school, be polite to adults, and become what we used to refer to as well rounded, or accomplished in many areas beside academics. I did well in sports. I learned to be responsible and considerate of others. I learned not to annoy my parents (though this practice often fell short of the intention). I learned to care about and take care of others, particularly those I deemed less fortunate. I excelled academically, was pleasant and well liked by my parents and their friends, made friends easily and developed a strong social conscience that led me to become active in the anti-apartheid movement at a young age. I sailed into medical school, became a doctor, and later specialized in psychiatry.

I married and had children, worked hard, provided amply for my family, and, to all outward appearances, seemed to thrive and prosper. When cracks appeared in my competent and confident front, I found it relatively easy to paper over them. The world had no shortage of causes to which I could contribute.

Some years after leaving South Africa for Canada, things began to falter. I was thousands of miles away from my previous sources of support, my family and friends, my networks. Problems arose and tensions grew. I felt increasingly unfulfilled at work and was having petty conflicts with some colleagues. I felt self-righteously competitive with them in a way that led to conflicts in which I invariably came off second-best. Meanwhile, I was striving to provide for my family, but there seemed to be little acknowledgement and even less creative use of the opportunities I provided for them. My children became indifferent to their education and disruptive at school, which was anathema to me, given the extremely high value I placed on learning and the role of education in preparing oneself for a productive and self-sufficient life.

I was rapidly exhausting my repertoire of solutions to these growing problems. As the gap between problems and solutions grew, I found myself becoming more and more part of the problem and less and less part of the solution.

On one notable occasion, in a pathetic attempt to stay on my teenage daughter's good side and seem cool to her, I withheld important information from my wife about her disturbing behavior. In other words, I betrayed my parental role in order to remain friends with my daughter. My wife was dismayed and told me that my behavior was unacceptable. My neediness had become a burden. I was alarmed by this turn of events and went to see a psychotherapist, though not for the first time.

THERAPY

My earlier forays into therapy had been unproductive, because I always maintained the illusion that there was nothing essentially wrong with me. My problems were caused by circumstances mostly beyond my control, and the purpose of therapy was to clarify who (that is, my parents) had caused me these difficulties, how, and why. The role of the therapists was to reinforce my distorted views of why I was so troubled, not challenge them. I was not interested in facing up to how things were not right with me, and I likely would have stopped therapy had the focus been on my own responsibility for my problems.

It always seemed that any difficulties I had were because of what others did. It was not me who needed to change for me to be okay, but rather others who needed to change. This was true whether it was my parents, my wife, my children, my colleagues, officials, strangers, or friends. It was always up to someone else to be different for me to be okay. Therapy was the place for others to change, and by and large the therapists I saw did not disabuse me of this notion.

When I returned to therapy this time, I felt I was in deep trouble. I still held fast to the idea that it was others who needed to change, and I felt I had run out of ways to induce them to do so. My mounting distress combined with the perseverance and expertise of my therapist (I was very lucky to have found him) meant that I stayed in therapy long enough to begin to learn important truths about myself.

I learned that my experience of being insufficiently loved (as opposed to the reality of being more than sufficiently loved) was valid simply because it was my experience. This epiphany came when my therapist referred to my experience of being insufficiently loved as a "holocaust." Both he and I knew that it was a gross exaggeration to talk about my experience and that vilest of evils in the same breath. But what he conveyed in using that hyperbolic term was an understanding that my sense of dread that at any moment I could be cut off from the love, care, and safety of belonging—unless I kept being pleasing—was very real.

My experience of the tenuousness of belonging was valid simply because I experienced it, not because it was objectively true. It was sufficient to experience something and draw conclusions from it for it to be valid. In the world of the emotions, subjective experience was all that mattered. Objective truth was of no, or certainly of lesser, importance.

My therapist never suggested or reinforced my notion that my parents had been deficient, but rather endorsed my experience of insecurity as being valid. Moreover, the discrepancy between my experience and the reality was not a sign of illness; on the contrary, I learned it was natural for this kind of discrepancy to exist between the perceptions of a child and objective reality. I came to understand that I would have had the experience of being unlovable regardless of whether I had or hadn't been loved.

In this way, this long-standing source of disabling self-doubt about the discrepancy between my feelings about my childhood and the reality of it was removed. Now, instead of wasting my energies focusing on the past, I was free to examine what was not working in my present life and to figure out how to make it work better.

I overhauled my attitude, particularly toward my children. I learned to separate my sense of self-worth from my concerns. I learned that my worth was not a function of my or my children's achievements, performance, or behavior. I began to understand that their values and behavior were about them and not a reflection of me. I began to create and maintain healthy and appropriate boundaries between myself and my children as well as other people to whom I had previously entrusted my sense of worth. I learned that I could not make other people—not even my own children—be the way I needed them to be so that I could feel good about myself. I could not change my children, just as I could not change my parents. If I could not change my own children, it was hopeless to imagine that I could change anyone else.

I learned that the only things I could change were within me and that I had to come to terms with and make peace with the things that I could not change, things both within and beyond myself. What followed were significant changes in my life and in my relationships, all generally for the better. I felt freer—free from the compulsion to please others and freer to be the way I thought might be of interest to me. I felt increasingly secure and at peace with myself. I no longer needed to achieve to have self-worth. Achievement was now a choice and not an imperative. I felt happy with myself even if I was not happy about my circumstances. By this time I (mistakenly) thought I had learned all, or enough of, what there was to know about self-empowerment and personal growth. So I ended my relationship with my therapist on a good note.

THE PENNY FINALLY DROPS

Some time later I had the good fortune to attend a personal growth weekend seminar run by Landmark Education. It was the first time I had ever attended a personal growth seminar. I considered them flaky and not the sort of thing psychiatrists took part in. But I was so impressed with the very well-crafted and professionally presented approach to individual freedom and personal empowerment that I attended a more advanced seminar a year later in Seattle. At this seminar I experienced a breakthrough in understanding that can best be described as an epiphany. The circumstances of this epiphany still amuse me.

During the latter part of the seminar, I struggled to understand the concept of responsibility that the seminar leader, Barbi, was trying to convey. She was talking about being responsible for oneself. I thought of myself as a responsible person. I took my obligations seriously, had studied hard at school, worked hard to provide a comfortable living for my family, paid my bills, always showed up for my patients, and involved myself in different community causes (a bit like Zossel, without the religious parts).

My sense of responsibility extended into being responsible for others in the quaint, paternalistic way that is not uncommon in South

African culture, particularly among the privileged. I worked hard at taking care of others both within and beyond my family. Being responsible, I believed, was a crucial element of my identity. But when Barbi spoke of responsibility, I knew she was addressing something else. And I couldn't, for the life of me, understand what she was talking about.

I asked her for clarification. She took extra time to try to convey to me the concept of emotional responsibility and responsibility for oneself, but the idea remained elusive. The examples she used to explain the concept didn't resonate. One example was her account of riding in a car with her boyfriend, who drove recklessly. Barbi talked about how vulnerable she felt being a passenger in his car and how annoyed she got when he ignored her repeated requests to drive more carefully. She said that, after a while, she realized that her feelings of fear were actually about her, not about him. She realized that it was her choice to be with him, both in and out of the car, and that if she chose to be with him, she was choosing to be with him as he was. "Inconsiderate driver" was just one of the qualities she was choosing in choosing him. Therefore, in choosing him, she had no business nagging him about his driving, or anything else. She understood that no one was making her get into a car with him, let alone be with him. In short, she was responsible for her decisions about who she was with and who she allowed to drive her, while he was responsible for his decisions about, among other things, how he drove and the extent to which he took her wishes into account.

This was one of the examples of responsibility by which Barbi really meant emotional responsibility, the idea that she was responsible for her decisions. She had the freedom to make her decisions about who she wanted to be with and how to do things in her life. She had the freedom to choose and the responsibility to stand by her choices. As I recall, she chose to stay with him—though I don't know for how long.

Despite her explanations, I still missed the point. I could not reconcile my understanding of responsibility—the kind that was about meeting your obligations—with this other kind, which was about being responsible for your decisions, feelings, and actions. It didn't take much longer, though, for the penny to drop.

At the end of this intense weekend seminar, I was preparing to drive back to Vancouver with the aim of being back at work the next morning (I was responsible; I had work obligations to meet). But I could not find my keys. I searched every room I had been in during the weekend, but to no avail. I enlisted the help of event organizers and admin people, but they also came up empty-handed. I went to the restaurant I had eaten at earlier in the day, scoured the sidewalks I had walked, all to no avail.

My fantasy was that if my keys did not turn up, someone would graciously offer to take me back to my hotel and help me arrange to replace my keys so that I could leave early enough the next day to be back in time for work, for my patients. I noticed myself becoming disparaging of the people who were still present at the center—even those who were still helping to search—because they were not living up to the fantasy rescue scenario I was concocting. In the end, someone suggested I contact an emergency locksmith and provided me with some phone numbers. A locksmith eventually came out and fabricated a new key.

By two in the morning I was on my way home to Vancouver. While driving, I reflected on the weekend, on my difficulty understanding Barbi's concept of responsibility, and on my parting experience of losing my keys and how things had unfolded. I thought particularly about how I'd felt it wasn't my fault that my keys had gone missing. I had been careful in looking after my things during the course of the weekend (because I was such a responsible person) and had deliberately checked to make sure that all my stuff was in its place. I thought someone must have taken the keys, deliberately or inadvertently, and I tried to figure out why someone would do that to me and why they hadn't called the center once they discovered that the keys didn't belong to them. These thoughts absolved me from blame and had the effect of holding others responsible for my misfortune. It never occurred to me that I was not being responsible.

My musings were interrupted halfway home by a call on my cellphone. It was my then twenty-four-year-old daughter. She lives in Johannesburg and was en route to Vancouver for a visit. She was calling in a panic to say that she had been prevented from boarding her flight in London because her visa papers were not in order. She needed to go into London from Heathrow to get the proper stamps in her passport before being allowed to fly onto Vancouver. But she didn't have enough money to get the fast train into London or pay for the passport stamps. What's more, unless she could get the money immediately, she would be stuck in London, as the embassy was shortly due to close for a few days.

I bit my tongue and made arrangements to have the cash wired to her at the airport. Fortunately I didn't speak my mind. However, I was addressing her silently, giving her a lecture on responsibility, on how she needed to take care of her visa issues before she left home, on how she needed to make sure she had money for just these types of contingencies, and so on. It was a well-rehearsed monologue I'd had with her many times, mostly but not always in my own mind. I was right, of course, and also righteous in my attitude. After all, she was twenty-four, and it was high time she became responsible.

And that's when the penny dropped - the irony of me giving her heck for being so irresponsible about her visa and money, while feeling so strongly that I wasn't responsible for my missing keys, dawned on me. (By the way, those keys never did show up.) There I was, self-righteously lecturing her about something that, in the very same moment, I was ducking. It was a bolt of lightning that lit up the dark December sky. I understood then and there that I had been profoundly irresponsible in the matter of my keys. While I had gone through the motions of being calm and eventually doing what needed to be done to resolve the crisis, I had been blaming others—for taking my keys, for not replacing them for me, for not looking after me. By expecting others to come to my rescue, I was not taking responsibility.

I could now see the flaw in my thinking. While I had ultimately behaved responsibly by making the arrangements to replace the keys, I had not been emotionally responsible. What Barbi meant was that whatever happened to you, even and especially when it was events that were not under your control, you and only you are responsible for your reactions, feelings, and behavior. What mattered was not so much what happened or whose fault it was, but rather how you were with what was happening to you, which meant you taking responsibility for yourself, your feelings, your emotions, your words, your actions, your reactions—for everything that came from you in relation to whatever it was that happened.

You are not responsible for what happens around you or to you, but you are responsible for how you respond. Responsibility, then, is more than meeting your obligations; it is a state of mind in which you and only you are responsible for your emotions, your actions, and your reactions. Nobody else in the world is responsible for you and for your feelings. This is what I finally understood Barbi to mean by responsibility: the notion of responsibility for yourself, being responsible for how you are with what ever happens to you.

I shared this insight with my daughter when she finally arrived, rather than the well-rehearsed but now dated lecture on my former understanding of responsibility. Thanks to Barbi, my daughter received the upgraded version rather than the hackneyed one (though unfortunately still in the lecture format).

THE SHAPE OF ADULTHOOD

For much of my life I wondered what it would be like to be grown up. I remember thinking that it might happen when I started high school or when I had my bar mitzvah; perhaps when I graduated from university or when I had sex for the first time or when I took my first job, owned my first car; perhaps when I married or had my first child or took out my first mortgage or started my own practice. But no. All these events came and went, yet the sense of being grown up eluded me. When my father died and I was the only male in my immediate family left standing, I remember thinking that this was the time I would finally morph into an adult.

But I continued to feel as I always had, waiting for this mysterious and elusive sense of being an adult to come along. I continued going through the motions of behaving like an adult, without ever truly feeling like one. Nothing happened until that moment on the road to Vancouver. It was then that I finally got what it meant to be responsible for my life, and then when for the first time I understood what it meant to be an adult.

If adulthood means reaching the state where you become emotionally responsible for yourself and thus responsible for your sense of self-esteem, then it is something we all need to consciously learn, because the learning of this is neither instinctive nor automatic. Our cultural institutions do not teach us this. Our families, schools, religious and political institutions, the media all teach us just the opposite - they teach us how to please others, how to fit in and how to earn approval from others in order to be and to feel worthwhile. As long as others are responsible for our worth, we are not and so do not functioning as emotional adults, In this sense we need to teach ourselves how to make this transition into emotional maturity.

I will now share with you in detail the steps required to direct yourself actively toward emotional responsibility and emotional adulthood. It is my belief, drawn from both my own experiences and from those of patients I have worked with, that this journey can be purposefully mapped out and successfully completed using information and the motivation to apply the information in the direction of change.

CHAPTER 2

THE ORIGINS OF SELF-ESTEEM

"The greatest happiness is to know the source of unhappiness."

— *Dostoyevsky*

A HIGH ACHIEVER'S DEPRESSION: PHIL'S STORY

We are often surprised when we discover that people we admire—people who seem so confident and successful, people who seem to be on top of the world—can break down and collapse, and become what we now so easily refer to as depressed. Phil is a classic example of this.

Phil was a tall, handsome man in his late forties. He was a successful lawyer with his own practice. He was married with two children and had an elegant lifestyle, lacked for nothing, and was the envy of many who knew him. He came from humble origins and was self-made. He had put himself through university and established a thriving practice that was financially, intellectually, and professionally rewarding. He had a busy social life and was active in his community. He was a high achiever with a golden touch.

But underneath the façade of Phil's easygoing and effortless interpersonal style lay a personality that worked tremendously hard to make others—his clients, colleagues, staff, family and friends—happy. If he could make others happy, he thought, they would think well of him. As long as others thought well of him, he could think well of himself; he could feel worthwhile. The burden of keeping everyone happy was immense, and he hid the strain behind a competent and affable demeanor. But the stresses in his life had mounted over the preceding few years, and a situation that arose at his office proved to be the final straw.

A member of his staff had become domineering, and Phil had failed to stand up to him. Phil never liked conflict, but in this instance, he thought that he ought to have stood up to the staff member and provided leadership. He believed that his failure to deal directly with the situation had compromised the atmosphere in the office. He thought that he had lost the respect of his staff as a result.

Phil became overwhelmed and unable to cope. He lost confidence, focus, and eventually the ability to work. He began to ruminate about his perceived failure to provide leadership and maintain a congenial atmosphere in the office. He became fixated on his sense of failure, and this grew to the degree that he became unable to think about anything else. He developed morbid fantasies about losing his practice, his family, and his lifestyle. Life no longer seemed worth living, and he contemplated death. Acutely depressed, Phil left work and went on disability. He went to see his doctor, who put him on antidepressants. He then felt like even more of a failure for having to resort to pills.

Phil had been depressed for a year when he was referred to the mood disorder clinic, a specialist service at the University of British Columbia hospital, which is where I met and treated him. By that time, he had been treated with three different antidepressants. Though he achieved modest relief of some symptoms, he remained sad and unmotivated. He was constantly tired and could no longer enjoy his family or his many activities. He was unable to gear himself up to go back to work. He worried constantly and could not sleep at night. He was plagued with thoughts about not being good enough, about being a loser. He was afraid people would discover that he was an imposter and a failure, so he shunned company.

It soon became apparent that despite his many outward signs of success, Phil had a surprisingly fragile sense of self-worth. He thought that unless he impressed people, he wouldn't be noticed. To him, not being noticed and appreciated meant that he was not worth being noticed, that he was not worthwhile, that he was worthless. This was made poignantly explicit when he described events at a recent public meeting he attended. At one point, the organizers called on the audience for volunteers. Phil knew that he was already overcommitted, that he was in no position to volunteer, and that he ought to keep his hand down. At the same time, he felt as though the organizers were actually directing their call specifically to him, even though he knew rationally that this was not the case. In his mind, the meeting had been called so that he would volunteer, and everybody in the audience was waiting for him to do so. Against his better judgment, he felt compelled to volunteer because of his feeling, unrealistic as it was, that the entire meeting was all about him, that he had to do the right thing and that by volunteering, he would make everybody else happy, which meant to him that he would earn the approval and admiration of others. He was even more miserable after he raised his hand.

As we explored this incident, it emerged that he had been born into a poor but stable family. His father was austere and undemonstrative, and had high expectations of Phil. Phil's view was that he had been raised in a normal family, enjoyed an untroubled childhood, and, despite the lack of openly expressed affection, had never suffered unduly.

Phil was at a loss to explain why he was so sensitive to the opinions of others. Before the incident at his office and the ensuing depression, he had never given much thought to his dependence on the approval of others. As his crisis unfolded, he became increasingly aware of his deep need for approval and how fragile his sense of self-worth was without it. He became very interested in understanding how his need for approval, his self-esteem, and his depression were linked.

Through the course of treatment, he came to understand these connections and was able to acquire a healthy sense of self-worth that was not dependent on the opinion (or imagined opinion) of others. As this fell into place, his mood improved, the symptoms of depression evaporated, and he was able to quit taking the antidepressants.

THE UNIVERSAL NATURE OF LOW SELF-ESTEEM

In the case of Phil, low self-esteem was at the root of his unhappiness, depression, anxiety, and despair. And it seems from my experience that the vast majority of people who exhibit symptoms of depression and anxiety are struggling with low self-esteem. In fact, as I reflect back on my years working with patients, I can't think of many instances when someone with a genuinely healthy sense of self developed these symptoms and problems.

The connections between low self-esteem and depression seem fairly obvious. It is hard to imagine feeling happy when you think you're not good enough. So much anxiety comes from feeling inadequate and the accompanying fear that however hard you try to disguise your inadequacies with displays of competence, you will eventually be revealed to be of little worth.

I think that most people have low self-esteem, acquire it around the age of three, and that it emerges as part of normal, healthy emotional development. Most people arrive at the same conclusion during the course of normal development that they do not matter and are not worth caring about. This provokes a dilemma of how to be cared for, how to be in order to be cared for and how to become worthwhile. These dynamics play out so early in our lives that we cannot remember reaching the conclusion of our intrinsic worthlessness. And because we can't remember reaching this conclusion, we think that our low self-worth is a self-evident truth of almost cosmic proportions. Because we reached this conclusion so early we cannot and do not appreciate that we reached this conclusion ourselves and that we made up or invented the idea of our own worthlessness. We cannot appreciate that we formed this low opinion of ourselves at this early time in our lives when no other conclusion was possible.

Something important to bear in mind about this conclusion of our intrinsic worthlessness is this: we all reach this conclusion of our innate worthlessness irrespective of who our parents are or were and how they treated us; we formed the conviction of our worthlessness independent of the family we were born into, regardless of our gender, culture, or the era we were born into, and without regard to other random influences. We reached this conclusion based on the inescapable unfolding of specific and unavoidable psychological realities, and there is nothing that anyone—not even the most loving or informed parent—can or could have done do to prevent either the formative influences or the conclusions.

There are a number of specific circumstances that occur in the course of early development that lead us to this painful conclusion about our intrinsic lack of worth. Let us consider some of these early developments, while bearing in mind that when considering the emergence of self-esteem, that self-esteem is a quality of the self, and that we first need to examine the emergence of the self before investigating the emergence of self-esteem.

FUSION AND SEPARATION

One of the first of these lines of development to consider is the way in which you transform from being a creature fully fused with your mother, as you grow inside her during pregnancy, to becoming a separate creature living outside of her body. In the womb you are like a parasite living off your host, who in this case is your mother. Between you and your mother is a layer, the wall of the womb. But as a fetus, you are oblivious to this. If it were possible at this stage—which it isn't—to think and to understand your experience of this very early time in your life, you would understand that you were not a discreet, separate, and independent creature, but rather a part of someone else, a part of someone else's body and being, a part of someone else's self. You would understand that as long as you existed inside your mother, you were not your own separate self, because you were literally fused with and exist as a fused part of another self, the self that is your mother.

This state of fusion comes to a dramatic end at the moment of your birth, when you are expelled from your mother's womb and enter the world as a separate being. Once the umbilical cord is cut, you are literally separated from your mother in a way that can never be undone. You are now, for the first time in your experience, separate; you have become in that instant a separate being. In the process of being born, you have undergone a profound transition from being fused, from being a part of someone else's self, to becoming your own person, your own self. Of course you are not conscious of this pivotal shift in your status at the time. That awareness comes later.

While many people think that life begins at birth, many others think that life begins at conception. The life-beginning-at-birth view corresponds to the view of life as a separate, not a fused being, in contrast to the life-beginning-at-conception view which coincides with the view of life as a fused being that later becomes separate. Each view has its own legitimacy. If you take the life-beginning-at-conception view, then it is possible to think of the origins of your life starting even before conception. In his book The Selfish Gene, Richard Dawkins introduces the idea that genes live, and that life forms are merely gene transporters forms, ferrying the genes from one point, a point in time, to where they want to go, which is a future point in time. He raises the fascinating prospect of thinking about our selves from a genetic perspective in contrast to the personal way we customarily think of ourselves.

So if you think about your self from this genetic point of view, with the idea that you are the genetic material contained in the sperm and egg of your parents, you can appreciate that even before you were conceived, you existed as the genes that were in your mother and of your father; a genetic part of you existed in the cells of your mother and another part in the cells of your father. At conception, these different parts of you came together to become the fetus that grew into the you that you are now. In this sense, your fused existence did not begin at conception, but rather before conception, insofar as you were fused with both your mother and your father in the cells of their bodies. In other words, until you were born and someone cut the umbilical cord and you became separate, your existence was in the form of being fused with and a part of your two parents before conception and fused with your mother during gestation.

You can reason this way back to your genetic existence in the cells not only of your parents but also in the cells of your parents' parents. Just as you existed genetically in your parents before conception, so they existed genetically in their parents before their conception. The genetic you that existed in both your parents before conception also existed in all four of their parents before they were conceived, and so you can say that you existed genetically in your grandparents before both your and your parents' conception.

In this same way you can trace your existence, genetically speaking, all the way back to the beginning of humankind by imagining that before your conception, you existed literally as a part of all the individuals who came before your parents. You were present in the cells of every one of your ancestors, in the form of the chemical matter that makes up genes that existed inside the nuclei of certain cells inside their bodies. In this sense your existence prior to your actual birth has always been fused with other individuals. You have always been a part of other selves, and only once you are born and the cord is cut, for the first time in the extremely long history of your existence, you shift from being part of other selves to being your very own self. Considering your extensive history of being fused with other selves, the moment of your birth is indeed a dramatic and profound shift in your experience of life, in your existential reality. For the first time in your history, you are your own separate self.

It is not surprising, then, that it takes some time before you are able to appreciate that you have become a separate being and that it takes a while for the awareness of your separateness to catch up with the reality of being separate. It is not clear when precisely this awareness dawns but it is likely that it emerges gradually over time, in fits and starts, and eventually comes together in a way that is clear and irreversible. There eventually comes a time when you know yourself to be a distinct and separate being, no longer part of your mother, but irrefutably you, It is no longer possible to know yourself in any way other than as a separate person, as your own separate self.

THE ROLE OF THE TANTRUM

I think that if this knowledge and awareness of your separateness has not consolidated before you are two years old, then this is the age at which it does definitively fall into place. Children typically begin asserting themselves and becoming oppositional from their early twos. One of the ways they do this is by means of the well-known tantrum, which gives a clue to the falling-into-place of this self-knowledge. A tantrum is the child's way of expressing an opposing will. When the two-year-old child says no to her mother, she is saying that her will is different from her mother's. A tantrum is a particularly loud and eloquent behavioral expression of this difference of will or desire. If your will is different from your mother's, it follows that you must be different from her. You cannot be the same as her if your wills are different.

It is likely that some sense of being separate develops before this time of tantrums, but from the time children start having tantrums, they have no further doubt that they are distinct, different and separate from their mothers. They are able to appreciate that they are their own separate, individual human beings.

There is a delay between the reality and the awareness of being separate. This developmental arc of becoming separate and later becoming aware of being separate is key to appreciating the later emergence of low self-esteem—first, because it is the process of developing the self, of which self-worth is a quality and, second, because of the actual mechanism whereby you are able to know your separateness, which is the next subject for discussion.

COMPARING YOURSELF WITH OTHERS

To appreciate your separateness, to know that you are your own self, you need to be able to distinguish yourself from others. Remember that the first and only way you knew anything about yourself up until this point has been as a self fused with other selves. To be able to recognize your own separateness, you need to notice the differences between yourself and others, and the way you appreciate these differences is by comparing yourself to others.

To know yourself, to have any awareness of yourself, you must have some sort of picture of yourself. The "picture" you form is a sensory impression of yourself to which most of your senses contribute, but it's primarily visual. You hold up this picture of yourself and compare it with the visual images of others—your mother, initially—and notice the differences.

We all have the built-in ability to form an image of ourselves, to hold the image up and compare it with the images we form of other selves, and to notice the differences.

Since your mother is the first person since your birth that your identity is bound up with and the first person from whom you differentiate yourself, it makes sense that she is the first person against whom you compare yourself. And when you do, you notice the obvious ways in which you and she differ. You notice, for example, that she is bigger than you are. You notice other obvious differences, such as that she is stronger and smarter than you are, that she takes up more space, that she does things that you cannot, that she is more competent than you. In contrast to her, you recognize that you are small, weak, and incapable. In all the ways that you compare yourself to your mother, what you cannot help noticing is that you are less than she is, that you are inferior to her.

DIFFERENCES AND THE EMERGENCE OF SELF

It seems an inescapable aspect of animate life, at least from a certain level of evolutionary development onwards, that creatures have the ability to recognize differences between themselves and others and to make decisions about their behavior based on an appreciation of the observed differences. Without this ability for creatures to compare themselves to others, a smaller, weaker creature may well become the next meal of a larger, stronger, and hungrier creature, and so cease to exist. Dying in this way means that the genes carried by that creature do not get to where they want to go, which is to the next generation, and so the creature that cannot compare itself with others, that cannot detect differences is poorly equipped to carry out its primary function of gene transport and therefore life. This inability to compare therefore goes against the survival instinct and is incompatible with life, and so we can think of the imperative to compare ourselves to others and notice the differences, as a crucial survival tool.

Since life depends on passing on your genes to the next generation, being killed because you cannot notice differences—and therefore potential threats—makes it less likely that you will survive to the point where you can pass on your genes to the next generation. So, members of a species whose genes do not allow for the ability to compare themselves with others are not likely to pass their genes on and will thus be eliminated from the gene pool, whereas individuals whose genes allow for the ability to compare themselves to others will be more likely to survive dangers and more likely to survive and endure. So when you find yourself comparing yourself with others, remember that you are not vain or insecure, but rather that you are simply acting out a biological imperative, that it is merely your survival instinct, likely under genetic control, at work.

All essential life functions, not just survival from would-be predators depend on the capacity to compare and contrast yourself with others. Feeding, mating, and territoriality are some examples. Parental creatures need to be able to detect which young carry their genes in order to provide them at least preferentially, with food. I remember seeing mother seals in the Galapagos Islands a few years back shooing away baby seals and only feeding their own offspring. These mother seals had to be able to compare their pups with others to notice which ones to feed and therefore keep alive. In very obvious and self-evident ways, mating behavior requires the same capacity to compare self with others, and others with others, in order to select optimum breeding partners. Survival includes activities where competition, cooperation, and protection are vital. Without the capacity to compare—to notice differences as well as similarities—the ability to both compete and cooperate is severely compromised, and survival is at risk. Life without comparison is unthinkable.

INFERIORITY: FINDING MEANING IN DIFFERENCE

In considering this whole business of comparing yourself with others, you will appreciate that most, if not all, of us spend our lives comparing ourselves with others. We make ourselves miserable when we think that others are bigger, stronger, smarter, richer, more beautiful, sexier, thinner, healthier or happier than we perceive ourselves to be. We may even feel victimized by the advertising industry, which seems to throw in our faces all the myriad ways in which we compare so unfavorably to others—there is always someone bigger, stronger, faster, smarter, prettier, happier, healthier and wealthier than we are—so that we'll want to buy things to make us feel better about ourselves.

But we have to remember that the advertising industry did not invent the activity of comparing. This drive to compare came about long before advertisers did; it is biological. Just because advertisers exploit our tendency to compare ourselves unfavorably to others doesn't mean they invented it. Advertising merely exploits this drive in order to sell us stuff.

Snow White's stepmother didn't need the advertising industry to prompt her to murder in the famous fairy tale in which she compares herself to her stepdaughter and comes off second-best. Who can ever forget her desperate refrain of "Mirror, mirror on the wall/Who's the fairest of them all?" or the homicidal rage she flew into when the mirror answered that it was her stepdaughter, not her. The mirror, of course, told her the truth: that there is always someone more beautiful (or rich or handsome or funny or whatever). But the most important thing in her life was to be fairer than her stepdaughter—than all other women—so she constantly made the comparison and structured her life around being the "fairest one of all."

Our comparing faculties are deeply ingrained in our psyches and from the very outset see ourselves as less than our mothers and become adept at seeing ourselves as being less than others. We don't need help from anyone—or a magic mirror—in comparing ourselves negatively with others.

So, you first compare yourself with your mother when you are two years old and notice the obvious differences: she is bigger, stronger, and smarter than you are. As you look beyond your mother and notice others in your environment and compare yourself to them also, you notice that everyone else stands in the same relation to you as your mother does: everyone else is also bigger, stronger, and smarter than you are. So, what you can't help noticing is that you are the smallest, weakest, dumbest, and most incompetent self around. (Presumably, the only exception to this observation is if you have a younger sibling, who would, on the basis of your comparison, be the only smaller, weaker, and stupider person than you.) In recognizing yourself in relation to others, you see that you are less than not just your mother, but less than just every other being you know. You recognize that you are inferior to everyone else in your world.

This very early piece of self-knowledge, almost the very first thing you ever know and are able to know about yourself, which is that you are inferior, gets you off to a great start if low self-esteem is the goal, which it just might be.

Fortunately, the formation of low self-esteem is not so straight-forward as to be based on the results of simple comparison. The unfavorable comparisons we make with others around us at the age of two are not the cause of low self-esteem. If that were the case, you would expect to acquire positive self-esteem as you grew enough and started to compare favorably with more and more people around you. As you grew bigger, stronger, and smarter than other people around you, you'd expect your self-esteem to rise and soar. But this is not what happens. We generally become bigger, stronger and more knowledgeable than most people around us once we become teen-agers, because there are always more children, and pre-teens in a community than adults. However self-esteem typically declines or even plummets in the teens rather than rise, and this for interesting reasons that we will examine later. The point is that self-esteem does not derive from the results of simple comparisons between how you stack up against others.

It is rather that this natural and biological drive to compare yourself with others as a basis for establishing your initial sense of self is important not because it leads to self-esteem, but rather because it prepares you for the time when you later—and for entirely different reasons—form the view that you are worthless and that the self that is uniquely you is of no merit. You are receptive to the idea of your worthlessness because it is not an unfamiliar idea to you. It seems consistent with what you already know about yourself: that you are inferior to others. In developing your sense of self by comparing yourself with others and appreciating your inherent inferiority, you in a sense are priming and preparing yourself for the later understanding that you come to which is that this unique self of yours is not only inferior, but also worthless.

Inferiority and worthlessness are different but are also similar and can go hand in hand; they are internally consistent with each other. And because you already know yourself to be inferior, when you later reach the conclusion that you are worthless as well, the idea of your worthlessness is not entirely foreign to you, and it resonates with what you already know and have always known about yourself from as soon as you formed a concept of yourself as a separate being, which is that you are inferior.

In A Nutshell

- In the second or third year of life you finally recognize that you are a separate being by comparing yourself with others

- You notice that everyone else is bigger, stronger, more competent than you are

- You realize you are **less than** and **inferior** to others

- This realization of your inferiority is one of the earliest things you ever come to know about yourself

CHAPTER 3

THE CHANGING NATURE OF NEED

"There are children in the morning / They are leaning out for love / And they will lean that way forever."

— *Leonard Cohen, Suzanne*

THE HEAVENLY WOMB

Consider this: while you are in your mother's womb, you have everything you need. You have a place to stay, a warm and cozy environment that is quiet and peaceful. You float in a sea of blissful tranquility, a sea that insulates you from jarring noises and other startling stimuli. You hear the gentle, soothing rhythm of your mother's heartbeat. All your nutrients are piped in constantly so you experience no hunger and know no pain or discomfort. Your every need is anticipated and met without you having to lift a finger. You lack for nothing. You don't even know you have needs because whatever you need is anticipated and met before it has a chance to reach your awareness,

You experience the contentment of needs that are all met and remain in this state until you are born.

The womb is an ideal environment, even though sometimes things can and do go wrong. Often when things go wrong—which means that the fetus' needs are not met—the situation may become incompatible with life, and the fetus perishes. It is also possible for things to go wrong to a lesser degree, to a degree that is not life threatening, where the fetus survives the pregnancy even though conditions were not ideal and the fetus' needs went unmet and it suffered. Overall, though, it can be said that for the most part, the experience of the womb is that it is an ideal environment, a place where all of the fetus' needs are met without it ever being aware that it needs anything, a place where it does not experience pain, discomfort or distress, a place where, before birth, it is at perfect peace.

This experience of the ideal, of perfection, of having no needs and knowing no pain or discomfort, is very similar—if not identical—to many of the ideas we form in our cultures of a perfect place we return to after we die.

Heaven is conceived of (no pun intended) as a place where there are no needs, where there is nothing to do or think about, where there are no problems to solve. There are no shopping malls or traffic jams, no washing to hang or shirts to iron, no meals to prepare or dishes to wash, no cars to repair, no lawns to mow, no queues to stand in, no wages to be earned, no taxes to be paid. There is no hunger, no crime, no punishment. Heaven is almost by definition a place where there is no pain or suffering; it is the place where suffering ends (or so it seems in the popular imagination and common renditions of heaven).

Nirvana shares similarities with this womb-like state of being. One of the key elements of the nirvana state is that there are no needs, no cravings or attachments, and thus no suffering. It is a sea of tranquility much like the amniotic sea of the womb. Paradise and the garden of Eden are places in our imaginations that hearken back to the womb experience, where everything we need is provided, where there is nothing to do and no needs to be met, where pain, longing, and suffering do not exist.

Of course there is much more to be said—and that has been said—about the notions of heaven, paradise, nirvana, and so forth, but for our purposes, it is enough to recognize the similarities between the universal womb experience and the idealized, womb-like ideas of perfection that crop up in so many cultures.

It is well known that from a mother's point of view, giving birth is excruciatingly painful. The pain of childbirth is sometimes used as a yardstick to measure the extremes of pain: it is sometimes said that something is as bad or worse than childbirth. From the infant's point of view, we can reasonably imagine that the process of birth is at the very least uncomfortable, but at the very most much worse. Even in the absence of complications, passing through a very narrow space over a period of hours—after floating for so long in the roomy womb—is likely unpleasant and shocking, maybe even traumatic. And then, at the moment of birth, you suddenly enter the world and experience a highly specific need for oxygen. For the first time in your experience, you need to breathe, because you no longer have your oxygen needs met by your mother and because life is not possible without oxygen in your lungs. So the first action you take, the first thing you do after being born, is breathe.

You may need someone to help you take a breath—the proverbial smack on the bottom—to get you going. That first cry starts your breathing, and from then on you're on your own as far as breathing goes, you meet your own need for oxygen. As long as you are able to breath, you live (at least this was true before the age of the iron lung and respirators). When you are no longer able to breathe, your life ends and you die. It is probably not surprising that your first act of life is a cry of distress. You are marking your expulsion from paradise with a roar of disapproval.

THE DISCOVERY OF NEED

You are born. Paradise is lost. Life has begun. You are now responsible for your breathing. By this act of being born and coming into the world, you are transformed from a creature with no needs to one with very distinct needs. Breathing is the first and last activity for which you are entirely responsible. For all your other needs you need the help of someone else.

Your life, your very existence, now depends on the satisfaction of these needs that before birth were met passively, but that now require the active intervention of others. Your life now depends on someone other than yourself to actively and intentionally meet your various needs.

Your mother is the other person who's job it to meet your needs and keep you alive. She is the primary other person you depend on to stay alive. If the sound of need is a distressed cry, then the sound of the alleviation of need is the comforting sound of 'mmmmm'. This 'mmmmm' sound is similar to the primordial vibration 'om' of Eastern religions that suggests a similar oceanic oneness, a peaceful unity of all things, an absence of discordance and pain. The word mother, at least in English, can then be seen as a combination of the sound 'mmmmm', this sound of the alleviation of need and pain, with the word 'other', the other person who induces alleviates your needs and this state of calm and peace.

In a sense, things get worse as you leave paradise further and further behind. In the womb you were never alone. You were always with your mother and it was not possible to be apart from her. But from the moment you are born, you separate from her and over time experience more and more separation from her, and spend more and more time apart from her. Separation is normal. It cannot be avoided. It happens spontaneously, inevitably and naturally. It happens regardless of how devoted, loving and attentive your mother is or isn't. A child separates from a devoted just as from a neglectful mother. Even though the circumstances of separation vary, all children separate from their mothers.

Even on the day of your birth, your mother is not as immediately available to you as she was before birth. You may be lying right next to her, but if she is asleep and does not respond to your call, it's as though she is not there and so you experience being separate from her.

As long as your needs are no longer anticipated or met, your mother is not present for you, either in reality or in the reality of your perception. The point is that after you are born, you can never be as close to your mother as you were when you were incubating in her womb. This has nothing to do with the kind of mother you had or how devoted or nurturing she was. The distance between the two of you arises simply because you are no longer part of her, and she is no longer able to meet your needs before you become aware of them.

What begins as moments of separation inevitably increases with the passage of time, the further away you get from the instant of your birth. You even begin sleeping further away from your mother and eventually in a separate space altogether. In this and in many other ways, you move further and further away from her. As time passes, you spend less and less time with her, especially when you consider the time and proximity you shared with her before you were born. In the normal course of events, as she goes about her daily activities—even activities that are centered around you—you are increasingly away from her, and there is nothing that can be done to alter this reality of your decreasing proximity to your mother. This growing separation from your mother is a normal part of healthy growth, development, and life.

The point about this growing loss of proximity from your mother is that you experience needs at different and unpredictable times of the day and night. You may develop a cramp, become hungry or cold, wet or soiled, or otherwise uncomfortable. You may be afraid of the dark and feel frightened when you wake up during the night. Because you are young, small and dependent, when you find yourself in a state of need, and cannot satisfy that need on your own, you need your mother to meet that need for you. And that's what she does; she meets your needs and alleviates the discomfort that accompanies your state of need.

However, the more you are apart from her, the more there are times when she does not respond to your call for help, and does not satisfy your need and so the more frequently you have the experience of needs not being immediately satisfied. It stands to reason that the less present she is when you need her, the less she will be able to meet your needs. This is unavoidable, regardless of the degree of care and attention that she gives you.

Bear in mind that during this early part of your life you have no sense of time or of the passage of time. You cannot distinguish between a minute and an hour, a day and several days. All you know is that when you are in a state of discomfort, you need it to be alleviated immediately—not in five minutes; you need it dealt with *now*.

HUMPTY DUMPTY AND THE EXPERIENCE OF UNMET NEEDS

How do you know when you're in a state of need and what is the experience of being in need? These are the next questions to be answered.

The state of need is experienced as a sensation, a physical or visceral sensation that has a slightly noxious or unpleasant quality. For example, you feel discomfort when you are hungry, thirsty, or need your diaper changed. This alerts you to the fact that you're in a state of need. This is one of the functions of feelings, to alert you to what is happening in your environment. For infants, there is a characteristic response to these unpleasant feelings, and that is to cry. Crying has the effect of alerting someone, usually the mother, to attend to the baby and alleviate its discomfort.

When your mother responds quickly and effectively, when she is able to satisfy your needs within a time frame that you can tolerate, your discomfort evaporates and is replaced by a state of calm. There is no more crying, just maybe a contented gurgle or sigh.

But what happens if that need is not alleviated, if the discomfort does not go away? The reason it does not go away does not matter early on, because all that matters, from your point of view, is that your discomfort persists. As the intensity of your discomfort increases, so the volume of your crying increases in your attempt to summon the help you now more urgently need. If your cries are successful, you receive the attention that alleviates your discomfort. If help does not arrive in time, your discomfort increases and may reach a pitch of severity that is painful. As a result, you yell even louder and louder until help finally arrives and your pain is alleviated.

This is a universal experience. Most of the time that you are in pain, you are able to summon help to alleviate that pain, but not always. And even if you succeed in summoning help, the help that arrives may not be enough to ease your discomfort, and your pain may persist even though your mother is there to help you.

The nature of pain is that it can be borne up to a certain point, but beyond that point, it can no longer be tolerated. Everyone has a pain threshold, or a point beyond which they cannot bear pain any longer. When you reach this point, you become overwhelmed. The language used to express the experience of being overwhelmed by the pain of unmet needs is the language of breakdown. We use phrases like, "I fell apart," "I cracked," "I fell to pieces," "I came apart at the seams," "I unraveled," "I shattered," "I was crushed," "I became unglued." All these expressions suggest an image of losing your sense of whole-ness and integrity, of no longer being a coherent single, solitary, inte-grated, unified being. Instead, the image is one of being broken.

A patient once described being overwhelmed as feeling as if she were strapped to a chair and whirling around so fast that her flesh flew off her bones. That's an extremely dramatic image of this state of being over-whelmed and falling apart in the face of unmet needs. But it emphasizes the nature of the intensely physical experience of losing your sense of integrity and wholeness when you hit your threshold of pain.

Humpty Dumpty captures this experience succinctly. You prob-ably remember how the nursery rhyme goes:

Humpty Dumpty sat on a wall

Humpty Dumpty had a great fall

All the king's horses and all the king's men

Couldn't put Humpty together again

No wonder the rhyme speaks so personally to us. Humpty Dumpty falls off a wall, hurts himself, and needs someone—his mother or father—to ease his pain and comfort him. The rhyme is as significant for what it does not say as for what it does: it says, "all the king's horses and all the king's men couldn't put Humpty together again." In other words, the pets and toys, the nursemaids, nannies, counselors, therapists and other hired help couldn't console him and make him better. Missing from the action, missing from Humpty's life at the moment he needs them most are the two people who can attend to his needs and soothe his pain, his parents, who in the rhyme would be the queen and king. They are absent, the king is mentioned only in passing and the queen not at all, and as a result, there is no comforting Humpty, there is no easing his pain, there is no making him whole again. The effects of the naturally occurring loss of proximity from his mother as he gets older and more independent is that she is no longer constantly present to meet his every need. As a result, Humpty, overwhelmed by his unmet needs, cracks up, and the life force seeps out of him, he bleeds to death at the bottom of the wall.

From Humpty's point of view, you can bring in all the king's horses and all the king's men, all the counselors and psychiatrists, all the priests and therapists, all the professional caregivers, child minders, nannies, and babysitters, clowns and heroes, stars and legends, all to no avail. Humpty needs his mother, and no one else will do. When she is not there for him when he needs her, he falls apart and cannot be consoled or put back together again. As he breaks apart, he bleeds to his psychological death; it's as though he dies emotionally. In the moment of being overwhelmed by his unmet needs, he experiences death.

It is my contention that everyone experiences Humpty Dumpty moments. It is a universal experience that cannot be avoided, no matter how loving and attentive your mother is. It happens because no mother can be present for her child continuously as they grow. And so, with the passing of time from birth, as your proximity to your mother diminishes, the likelihood increases that your mother will not be present when you need her, and that the discomfort of your unmet need will escalate to a point beyond that which you can bear. You will become overwhelmed and have a Humpty Dumpty moment, a moment that you experience like death.

This experience of being overwhelmed by unmet needs is the experience of abandonment. While we commonly think of abandonment as someone intentionally absenting themselves from a dependent, from Humpty's point of view, his mother's absence when he needs her is abandonment. There is a key difference between the adult and the child's notion of abandonment; for the adult, abandonment implies intention, whereas for the child, abandonment involves absence and the intentions of the mother are irrelevant.

Some children will endure more Humpty Dumpty abandonment experiences than others, for all sorts of reasons, some to do with their mothers and their family circumstances, some to do with themselves and the nature of their tolerances, activities, and unique needs. What matters is not how often you have these moments, but that you have them at all. My contention is that everybody does, and that it cannot be helped or avoided. At this early stage in your life, you are unable to compare your emotional experiences with those of others so that it is meaningless to you that your sibling or neighbor or anyone else has more or fewer Humpty Dumpty moments than you have; all that matters to you is that your needs go unmet, that you become overwhelmed, that you unravel and feel as though you die.

This death-like experience is not only deeply distressing, but also is experienced as a profound threat to your survival, to your very existence. This begs the next question: how do you deal with this threat to your life?

In A Nutshell

- In being born you leave the womb where all your needs are met without you having to do anything, and you enter the world where you have and experience needs

- Your mother is the person designated to meet your needs

- When your mother is absent, due to the normal process of separation, you fall apart and become overwhelmed by the pain of unmet needs – the 'Humpty Dumpty' experience of abandonment

CHAPTER 4

NARCISSISM AND COGNITIVE DEVELOPMENT

"Knowing others is wisdom; knowing yourself is enlightenment."

— *Lao Tzu*

All living creatures have ways of responding to threat. Life forms that do not or cannot respond to threat cannot sustain life and therefore cannot survive. We can assume that species of creatures alive today have ways of both detecting and dealing with threats to their integrity and that they can do so successfully enough to ensure their survival.

Different species have different ways of responding to threat, and humans have their own ways as well. When you think about it, humans are not particularly strong or swift and don't have big enough teeth or claws to deal with many of the potential threats to their survival. Humans do not see well enough in the dark to be nocturnal nor can they camouflage themselves sufficiently to avoid detection, and thus danger.

Humankind's main strategy for survival is through thinking, understanding the nature of the threats they face, and figuring out ways to overcome or bypass them. Humans are known as *Homo sapiens*, or Man the Wise, a designation that refers to the primacy of thinking as the main survival mechanism. You would be correct to say that "sapiens" is something of an overstatement. It seems a bit grandiose, given innumerable and ceaseless examples that point to the very opposite of our supposed wisdom. It would be more accurate to refer to man as *Homo cognens*, Man the Thinker, rather than *Homo sapiens*, but that's another story.

Thus, humankind's primary defense or coping mechanism is understanding, which is achieved by thinking. Humans survive by thinking, and so we need to consider how the ability to think comes about, what its nature is and how it develops, and then we will consider how the process of this cognitive development applies to the problem of how to deal with the perceived threat to our survival when our needs go unmet.

Thinking is a faculty in the same vein as any other human faculty, much like the faculty of movement, for example. We all know that you crawl before you run and that the faculty of movement emerges in an organized and staged fashion starting with the most elementary of abilities: in the beginning, you are unable to lift your head off the horizontal. But after developing through different stages, you reach the point where you can perform all sorts of highly skilled actions, like sewing a button, fashioning a pot from clay, driving a car, skating, performing microsurgery by remote control, or playing the piano.

No one is born playing a concerto on the piano or performing microsurgery, but latent within everyone are the abilities to perform highly complex and refined movements and actions. To realize these potentials, you necessarily grow through a series of steps whereby more and more of those latent abilities unfold and are brought into play. You develop by building on each step until the next stage is ready to unfold, and you then apply yourself to mastering this new stage. So it goes until you have fully mastered the latent abilities within you.

Thinking, like movement, is also a latent faculty within us and begins in a highly primitive form. It is so primitive in its earliest forms that we generally do not recognize these earliest expressions of mental activity as thought. Electrodes on the scalp of a fetus produce a tracing of electrical activity that reflects mental activity. Even though the electrical tracing has particular form and shape, and is recognizable as an electroencephalogram, this mental output of the fetus is not recognizable as thought. We may consider that babies do not think when they are in the womb, and as already discussed, there is likely nothing for them to think about, since all their needs are met.

The brain grows both in terms of the number of brain cells (neurons) and in terms of the connections between them (synapses). Much of this brain growth happens in the later stages of pregnancy, but even more explosively after birth. As this happens, the nature of the mental activity that accompanies this growth changes and becomes more coherent and more recognizable as thought. Even so, what we identify as thought and certainly the expression of thought takes some time to emerge. Most of us cannot remember anything from our early years because our memory systems—an important component of the thought apparatus—have not developed sufficiently to allow us to remember events or anything as abstract as thoughts.

It takes quite some time before humans become capable of remembering, of laying down and storing memories in ways that can be accessed later. The way that thinking happens in these earliest stages of life is so different from the coherent and meaningful ways we think later and so chaotic, disorganized, and illogical that, even if it were possible to remember those earliest experiences, it likely wouldn't make much sense.

It is possible to get a sense of how chaotic those earlier thought experiences might have been from our dreams since dreams can be a manifestation of developmentally primitive forms of thought. In dreams, the usual rules of logic, time sequence, continuity of character and plot often do not apply. Events unfold in haphazard ways and time sequence is random; there is not necessarily a beginning, middle, or end to the dream. It is often difficult or impossible to make heads or tails of a dream, and in this way, dreams offer a window into what your earliest thinking was like: jumbled, muddled, illogical, chaotic, difficult to remember, and difficult if not impossible to make sense of.

JEAN PIAGET AND COGNITIVE NARCISSISM

The great Swiss psychologist Jean Piaget described what he thought of as the essential aspects and processes of cognitive or intellectual development, the way and order in which different elements and abilities of cognition or thinking emerge from their latent state to a state where they are fully expressed. He outlined a number of different stages in the course of intellectual development, with each stage being characterized by the acquisition and emergence of specific cognitive skills.

Piaget described a specific intellectual function or skill that he thought emerged when children were around seven years of age, a process he called "decentering". The ability to decenter is the ability of a person to see things from a view other than their own, or to put themselves in someone else's shoes and see things from the other person's perspective and not just from their own. Before this ability to decenter emerges, children see things exclusively from their point of view. Piaget referred to this earlier way of thinking as egocentric, as cognitive egocentricity.

Piaget demonstrated egocentric and decentered thinking in the famous Three Mountain Problem experiment. He had children of different ages sit in front of a model of three mountains while he himself sat facing the model from a different direction so that his view of the mountains was from a different perspective than the childrens. He asked the children to describe what they saw from their own perspective, as well as what they thought he saw from his. The younger childrens' responses were that their view and Piaget's view were the same, while the older children correctly identified Piaget's perspective as being different from theirs.

This demonstrated to him that younger children were not able to put themselves in a position other than the one they were actually in, that they could not adopt a perspective other than their own. This way of thinking in the younger children—who could not decenter, who could only understand things subjectively—he described as cognitive egocentricity. Once children reached an age of around seven, they spontaneously and naturally acquired the ability to decenter—to see things from a perspective other than their own, to see things objectively.

It is almost thirty years since I was a psychiatry student in Johannesburg that a psychology lecturer described an experiment that demonstrated this process of decentering in a different and simpler way. The experimenter placed a dollhouse in front of children of different ages and asked them to draw what they saw. All the children drew the front view picture of the dollhouse as it appeared to them. He then asked them to remain in their seats and draw the house from the back. The children aged seven and older drew imaginative drawings of what they imagined, or thought, the back of the house might look like. The younger children drew what they saw, which was the front of the house.

The younger children drew only what they could see, which was the front of the house; they could only reproduce their original drawing. They were not able to imagine a view of the house that was different from their own, they could not perceive anything other than their own immediate and direct experience. As far as these younger children were concerned, they could not see the back of the house so it did not exist because they could not see it; to them there was no such thing as the back of the house; because it was not of their experience. For the older children who had acquired the capacity to decenter, and so were able to use their imaginations to experience things that they didn't experience directly themselves, the back of the house did exist—it existed in their imagination, and they could therefore relate to it and produce a drawing of the back of the house from how it appeared in their imaginations.

This experiment demonstrates again that the younger children had not yet acquired the ability to decenter, while the older children had. The younger children were cognitively egocentric, while the older ones had clearly left this stage of development behind and were capable of greater cognitive powers because this capacity to decenter opens the door to being able to use imagination as a cognitive tool and represents a great step forward in a child's intellectual development.

Because this is such an important issue, I will summarize and repeat it: children who cannot decenter have not yet acquired and therefore lack the imagination to see things from a perspective different from their own; they are in a pre-imaginative stage of cognitive development. Their thinking is egocentric. This means that they can only know what they experience directly themselves. What they do not experience directly, as far as they are concerned, does not exist. To them, there is no such thing as the back of the house because they do not experience it directly themselves. There is no such thing as someone else's point of view because they do not and cannot yet experience anything from a point of view other than their own. They can understand and appreciate experience only from their point of view. No one else's point of view exists, let alone matters. To the cognitively egocentric child, they are always the center of their experience, and since only what they experience exists, they are the center of their universe, which means to them—because they cannot imagine or know anything besides their own immediate experience—that they are the center of *the* universe. I prefer to call this egocentric thinking narcissistic thinking or cognitive narcissism.

Narcissism in this context refers to a worldview in which you are the center of the universe because you are at the center of *your* universe. In your mind the only universe that exists is the universe you experience. You cannot imagine anything beyond your own experience, so everything you experience relates to, and is about, you. You are the center of everything that you experience, which in your mind is the same as being the center of everything that happens. Of course this is not true since things happen around you that do not affect you and that you are not aware of, things exist beyond your experience of them, but to the mind of the young child who is not yet able to decenter, these things that they do not experience do not exist. In this state of mind, whatever happens to you is therefore about you. This is a very distorted view of reality but is the way children think and make sense of their experience before they acquire the intellectual capacity to decenter.

Let's look at what this means concretely for the pre-imaginative, pre-decentered child. When you are three and your mother is upset, you think that you are responsible for her state of upset because you cannot imagine anything else in her life other than you, and therefore you cannot know of any reason for her to be upset other than you. You cannot imagine anything in her life other than your experience of her life, which is about you. Everything you experience is about you, even the experience of other people and their emotions. Your mother's state of mind, be it her displeasure, joy, or indifference, is about you.

This is the only way that you can make sense of it. You do not yet have the intellectual understanding to think that her state of upset could be caused by something else, by something other than you. The real reasons for her being upset—maybe a tiff with your father, a negative encounter with a neighbor, a financial worry—mean nothing to you because you do not experience them directly yourself. Since you cannot imagine things that you do not experience firsthand, the tiff that you were not party to does not exist, nor does your mother's financial worries. Your cognitive narcissism makes you the center of everything that happens; whatever you experience is about you, so your mother's upset is about you, which means that you are the cause of her upset because you know nothing about the real causes of her upset. Once you are older and can decenter, you can then understand that there are other reasons for her state of mind, reasons that have nothing to do with you, but you can't understand this when you are three or four and have not yet acquired the capacity to decenter.

Here's a classic example of cognitive narcissism – in former times humans looked at the horizon and saw it was a flat line. They concluded that the world was flat, because the world appeared to them to have an edge, so it must be flat, and they were afraid they might fall off the edge if they sailed too far from shore. When astronomers later showed that the world was round, all but the members of the flat earth society could understand that the world was in fact round despite it's flat appearance. Another compelling example of this cognitive narcissism is mankind's earlier view that the sun revolved around the earth and that the earth was therefore the centre of the universe. This is because we observe the sun moving around us, rising in the east and setting in the west, as we remain stationary, so we think, or thought that the sun moved or revolved around us, which meant that we were the centre of the universe. Galileo showed that despite appearances, the converse was true, that we revolve around the sun and not vice versa.

Both these earlier beliefs are examples of the workings of cognitive narcissism, that how we experience things is how they are because, until we have better information and until we are able to understand and think about our experience objectively, what happens to us is about us, and that reality is subjective or personal. These great illustrations of the workings of cognitive narcissism also demonstrate the inaccuracies and distortions that flow from this form of more primitive narcissistic thinking.

It is probable that this cognitive narcissism comes on stream from around age three and remains your primary way of understanding your experience and thinking until decentering kicks in at around age seven.

This narcissistic way of knowing is the key to the formation of your self-esteem.

ABANDONMENT AND THE CONSTRUCTION OF SELF-ESTEEM

Probably by the time you are three, you have developed sufficient intellectual horsepower to make sense of some of your experiences, particularly the Humpty Dumpty moments where you feel that you are breaking down, falling apart, and at risk of dying, as I described earlier. By this age you have enough understanding to be able to explain your experience of falling apart to yourself, although at this early time, you still think narcissistically and your understanding is distorted by this intellectual narcissism, by your view that everything you experience is about you.

In applying this narcissistic way of understanding to the question of your needs being met or unmet by your mother, your three-year-old mind tells you that you are responsible for whether they are met or not. This is because you cannot understand that your mother has her own reasons for meeting or not meeting your needs, reasons that have nothing to do with you. At this stage you are as unable to know anything about maternal instinct or maternal love, or any other reason your mother might have for attending to your needs, just as you are unable to appreciate the reasons why she is not present for you when you need her.

Since you cannot imagine (or know) what you do not experience directly yourself, her real reasons for caring for you do not exist and so mean nothing to you; your only way to understand her caring for you is on your terms. In other words, her caring for you is about you and not about her. This is how you understand your experience when you are three and in this narcissistic stage of cognitive development. You attribute to yourself her reasons for meeting your needs. This is what it means to think narcissistically or to be cognitively egocentric.

By the same token, when your mother is not present to meet your needs and you become overwhelmed by the distress of her absence, you also attribute her absence to you and not to her. Since you are egocentric and cannot understand anything you do not experience directly, and you don't experience the reasons for her absence, you cannot and do not know the real reasons for her not meeting your needs. You cannot and do not know anything about traffic jams or work obligations or line ups at the supermarket or any of the other possible real reasons that she is absent at the very moment you need her. You cannot see the reasons for her absence from her point of view because you are cognitively narcissistic and can only see it from your point of view, which is that her absence is about you, not her.

Since her absence when you need her is about you and not for any real reason, this can only mean to your narcissistic pre-decentering mind that you do not matter enough to her for her to be present for you, that you are not sufficiently worth her while for her to be there when you need her. Your narcissistic interpretation of her absence in your Humpty Dumpty moments is that you do not matter, that you are not worth her while, and that you are not worthwhile.

The converse is also true: you make sense of her presence as being about you not her, which means to you that when she is there for you especially when you need her, her presence means that you are worth caring about, that you are worth her while, that you are worthwhile. Her showing up for you is about you, not about her; you matter enough that she shows up for you.

The way your narcissistic mind works is that if you are cared for, it's because you are worth being cared for, and if you are not, it's because you are not worth being cared for - simple as that.

This way of interpreting her presence or absence when you need her is the origin of self-esteem, is how self-esteem comes about. Self-esteem is the way you regard yourself as either being worth your mother's while to care for you and keep you safe and alive, to be present for you when you need her to meet your needs—or not. When she meets your needs, you make this experience mean that you matter to her, that you are worthwhile. And when she doesn't meet your needs, you conclude the opposite, that it's because you do not matter to her, that you are not worthwhile.

So how do you reconcile these different and opposing experiences of having your needs met at some times (in fact, most of the time) and not at others? How can you be worth caring about at some times but not at others? How does your three-year-old mind deal with the contradictions of being worthwhile some of the time and worthless at others?

Given that under normal circumstances you mostly have your needs met in a timely manner—and therefore enjoy the sense of well-being and of being worthwhile that comes with being cared for—you have plenty of opportunity to experience yourself as worthwhile. Since your needs are mostly met, and Humpty Dumpty moments are relatively infrequent, you can imagine that you would reach the conclusion that overall you are worthwhile because most of the time you are cared for and so are mostly worth being cared for, and are therefore mostly worthwhile. But since being worthwhile means being cared for and safe, if you are worthwhile there is not much for you to do to remain worthwhile: whereas if you are not worthwhile, not worth being cared for, then you will be motivated to do something to make sure you are cared for in order to make sure that you are kept safe and alive.

From the point of view of your survival it makes more sense to conclude that you are worthless because this conclusion motivates you to do something to make sure you receive care. You are motivated to find ways to make sure you are cared for and remain safe, in ways that you are less likely to be prompted to develop if you regard yourself as worthwhile, worth being cared for and so have no motivation to do anything to ensure your care and survival.

So you side with your less common experience of not being worthwhile rather than the more frequent one of being worthwhile, because being worthless prompts you to action to make sure you receive care, and this is a more adaptive way of ensuring your survival than deciding you are inherently worthwhile, because there's much less incentive to do anything to receive care if you are inherently worth being cared for.

In this way, you formulate your self-esteem and reach the conclusion that you are inherently not worthwhile, or are worthless. Because all children have mothers who are sometimes absent, and all children evolve through the stage of cognitive egocentricity before being able to decenter and think realistically, I propose that all children reach the conclusion at around the age of three that they are inherently worthless and not worth being cared for because of their inescapable Humpty Dumpty experience of sometimes not receiving the care they need at the time they need it.

It may happen, rarely, that for some children the timing of the question of why their needs aren't met is delayed and that they first come to ponder this question only once they're older and have the ability to decenter and so can be realistic and objective. Under these circumstances, the accurate explanation for their mothers' absence is realistic and not about them and so they will not draw this conclusion of their inherent lack of worth. There is no reason to conclude that you are worthless and you are then free to conclude that you are worthwhile. This might represent the exception to the rule, and be the rare and unusual state of innate high self-esteem.

So this approach presents a new way of looking at and understanding self-esteem, what it is and how it comes about. In this approach, two separate and unrelated strands come together to explain how you reach this conviction of your worthlessness—namely, your mother's unavoidable absence that leads to you feeling overwhelmed and abandoned, and your cognitive development that includes an egocentric or narcissistic way of understanding things before you are seven, that has you believe that whatever happens to you is about you, thus your mother's absences when you need her are because of you, not her, which in turn means that she is absent because you are not worth her while, that you are not worthwhile. This is how self-esteem comes about, and specifically how self-esteem comes about in the form of low self-esteem. This is the source of your low self-esteem, arising from your narcissistic explanation of your experience of abandonment. This is the only way you have at this stage of your life to make any sense of the recurring experience of your needs not being met. This is true for just about everyone else as it is for you, because all children have mothers who are not constantly present for them, and because all children develop through a stage of cognitive narcissism. This means that low self-esteem is a universal condition that affects all children and people throughout human history and occurs independently and regardless of each individual's unique circumstances. It is as true for how self-esteem comes about in children growing up in wealthy modern families and neighborhoods as it is for kids growing up in impoverished communities, as true for kids today as it was for kids hundreds and thousands of years ago.

This is a very different perspective on the origins of self-esteem—especially low self-esteem—from the prevailing view, which is that self-esteem results from how you are treated as a child: if you are supported and encouraged in childhood you emerge into adulthood with positive self-esteem and a positive sense of your self worth, whereas if you grow up in a circumstances where you are criticized, undermined and not supported you enter your adult life with low self-esteem.

In A Nutshell

- Thinking capacity develops along the lines of Jean Piaget's theory of Cognitive Development

- Between ages three and seven normal thinking is egocentric or narcissistic

- From age seven you are able to 'decenter', meaning you can see things from a point of view other than your own – (you no longer think only narcissistically)

- Until you are able to 'decenter', the only way to understand your mother's absence when you need her is narcissistically, meaning that her absence is about you

- To the narcissistic mind this means that if you're not cared for, it's because you're not worth being cared for, which means that you are worthless

- Thus self-esteem arises as low self-esteem before you are seven years old because of the (relatively few) times that you do not receive care and conclude (wrongly) that you are not worth being cared for, that you are worthless

CHAPTER 5

LOW SELF-ESTEEM AND THE IMPERATIVE TO PLEASE

"Please, please me, whoa yeah / Like I please you"

— *The Beatles, "Please, Please Me"*

The experience of being cared for and having your needs met in an acceptable time frame is, in your narcissistic mind, synonymous with the idea of being worthwhile. When your mother attends to you, your three-year-old mind takes it to mean that you are worth your mother's while. Conversely, when your needs are not met, you take this to mean that you are not worth having your needs met. Under the distorting influence of narcissistic thinking, you understand your needs being met or unmet as something related to your self-worth. Your ability to think of yourself as worthwhile is therefore derived directly from the experience of having your needs met by someone other than yourself, since this is happening at a stage in your life when you are unable to meet your own needs.

You are worthwhile only when your mother shows up to attend to you, because her presence, in your mind, means that you are worth attending to. Your worth, your intrinsic sense of value as a living being, is determined by your mother's attention to and care of you. Therefore, your understanding of your value is that it is determined not by you but by someone else, by a self other than you. In other words, you do not determine your value yourself; your mother does, through her actions toward you. Your understanding of your self-worth is that it is determined by the actions of someone else toward you and not by you yourself.

This means that the notion of your self-worth is not an abstract idea derived from an existential contemplation of your intrinsic value—since this is not yet possible for you to grasp at this early stage in your intellectual development that precedes your ability to think abstractly and philosophically. Rather, your self-worth comes from the way the important people that you depend on behave toward you and the narcissistically distorted way you understand their behavior.

Your conviction of your inherent worthlessness is probably reinforced to some degree by your earlier observations about being inferior to, and smaller, weaker, and dumber than everyone else around you. When you first made these observations, they did not cause you to think of yourself as worthless, as considerations of your intrinsic value were beyond your cognitive grasp at that time. But once the notion of self-worth is within your conceptual grasp, the idea that you are not worth caring about is not entirely unfamiliar, because you are already acquainted with the idea of being inferior dating back to the earliest time you acquired a sense of yourself as a separate being.

Regardless of the specifics of your actual experience of how caring or neglectful your mother was toward you, you reach the same conclusion that you are fundamentally not worth caring about.

Arising from the unavoidable experience of unmet needs and of your narcissistic way of thinking about your experience at the time you first begin to formulate notions of self-worth, you have no alternative but to reach the conclusion that you are inherently worthless, or not worth being cared for because of the times when you do not receive care. This understanding probably falls into place when you are around the age of three.

You emerge from your threes with the understanding that you are unworthy, unlovable, and do not matter. Nobody tells you, or needs to tell you, that you are worthless. Even if they do, it would only reinforce what you have already decided about yourself, and conversely, if you are told repeatedly that you are precious and that you matter greatly, you still reach this same conclusion of your inherent worthlessness. Furthermore, you don't remember deciding that you were worthless or that it was you who decided that you were worthless. So you accept this belief, this conviction, as though it were actually true, as true as gravity or any other cosmic or existential truth.

Even though your needs were met more often than not, it was still more adaptive for you to reach the conclusion about your worth based on the times when your needs were not met rather than when they were. You are better prepared for existential danger on the basis of a belief that you are intrinsically worthless rather than that you are intrinsically worthwhile. This is because you are spurred to find a solution to your worthlessness as a means of self-protection in a way that you would not be if you had decided that you were worthwhile.

To the three-year-old you, unmet needs, abandonment, and vulnerability mean worthlessness, which in turn mean threat and mortal danger. Identifying yourself as worthless means that you recognize the threat to your existence and are prompted to do something about it. Deciding that you are worthwhile means that you are not under threat, and so there is no (or less) incentive to do anything to prepare yourself in case you are threatened.

You decided you were worthless so long ago that you cannot remember reaching this conclusion. Because you cannot remember, it seems that the state of being worthless is something intrinsic, inherent, and, because of your narcissism, applies to you alone. Everybody else seems to be worthwhile; it is just you who is worthless. You cannot appreciate that it is not a cosmic truth about yourself, but rather something you decided about yourself before you knew any better. Having low self-esteem is something you made up so long ago and on such spurious narcissistic grounds that you cannot remember doing it.

IT DOESN'T MATTER WHAT THEY SAY

Jody's earliest memories were of her father telling her that she was useless and would never amount to anything. Her father was a drunk who made little of his life. Jody made numerous attempts at business and romance that, after initial success, failed. She became an alcoholic. She believed that she was useless and would never amount to anything. She thought her father was responsible for her thinking she was useless, and blamed him for her failures. She had no appreciation of her own role in coming to the belief of her intrinsic worthlessness.

Rosa was equally convinced of her intrinsic lack of worth and was so tormented by it that she was unable to continue working. But her father, in contrast to Jody's, had been a loving man who would wait for her after school to read to her, spend time with her, and show her things of interest. He was always encouraging. Neither he nor anyone else ever told her that she would not amount to anything. The only put-down she remembered happened in her early teens when a passing stranger made an unkind remark to her about her weight.

Yet in her adult life, Rosa made herself miserable second-guessing everything she said and did. She replayed conversations and interactions over and over in her mind, imagining that someone would find fault with her and see her for the failure she deep down believed herself to be. Her conviction about her inner worthlessness thrived in spite of all the positive and encouraging messages she had received throughout her life and in spite of her successes in her social, academic, romantic, and working life.

Despite having experienced very different childhoods, both Jody and Rosa suffered from low self-esteem. Rosa was no less convinced of her worthlessness than Jody was, despite the fact that her father was consistently supportive, affirming, and loving. His devotion to her no more protected her from low self-esteem than Jody's father's lack of devotion caused hers. In Rosa's mind, she never deserved her father's love and attention, and she felt sure that she would disappoint him and reveal to him that she was not worth loving. She was in constant dread that others would see through her façade of competence and discover the unworthy, incompetent person she believed herself to really be.

It is an enormous problem to live with the sense of not being good enough, for the simple reason that if you are not lovable, you will not be loved, if you are not worth being cared for, you can expect that you will not be cared for. And if you are not cared for—especially when your actual life experience is that you depend on others for your safety and survival—you will not be safe and you will not survive. Being unworthy or unlovable means that you are at risk of death because you do not deserve to be made safe. In a sense, being unworthy is synonymous with psychological death. The insecurity of thinking that you will not be cared for is intolerable. You are compelled as a matter of survival, by an instinct, to find a way to become worthy of being cared about so that you are able and more likely to survive.

As we have established, it is not within you simply to be worthwhile, because you have already decided that you are not. We have also seen that in order for you to feel worthwhile, it is up to your mother to treat you in a manner that you interpret as being worth her while. In other words, since your worthiness is determined by someone else—by your mother—you are driven to find ways to induce her to behave toward you as though you were worthwhile. You quickly discover that when you please her, she responds in a way that you understand to be caring, and when she cares for you, your experience is that you are worth being cared for. In other words, your negative self-esteem motivates you to find ways to please her so that she will be attentive to you, so that you can feel in those moments that you are worth being cared for. You then feel worthy and experience positive self-esteem.

Simply put, for you to feel or to be worthwhile, you have to please your mother. (Think of this as the pleasing principle, which is distinct from the pleasure principle. The pleasure principle suggests that your behavior is motivated by the search for pleasure, which is somewhat different from the drive and compulsion to please.)

Your ability to experience yourself as worthwhile therefore depends on the extent to which you can induce others to care for and value you, and your instinctive way of inducing others (your mother) to care for you is by pleasing, or trying to please them. The more you succeed at pleasing others, the more worthy and worthwhile you feel yourself to be.

Remember that your sense of externally derived positive self-esteem rests on your underlying conviction of an intrinsic lack of worth and so the positive self-esteem you derive from your mother by pleasing her may last a while, but will fade unless it is replenished by more and more gestures of approval and affection from her. The extent to which you can keep her validating your worth is the extent to which you are able to build a more lasting sense of positive self-esteem. The more you can elicit affirmation from her, the more your sense of positive self-worth grows. It may grow to be quite robust and dependable, or less so, depending on the circumstances of your relationship with her.

Pleasing your mother, then, is the absolute prerequisite for you being able to feel worthwhile and positive about yourself and is thus essential for your emotional well-being. As a pre-imaginative, dependent, narcissistic three-year-old, you grasp this imperative and take on the task of trying to please her. You use a trial-and-error method to discover what you can do to influence her attitude and demeanor toward you. You notice that some things you do coincide with her attitude or expression of approval, and you conclude—narcissistically, of course—that it is your behavior that makes your mother affectionate and affirming toward you.

When you connect a particular behavior of yours with the desired result from your mother, you are inclined to repeat it. If it again gives you positive results, you keep repeating it for as long as it continues to elicit the same positive result. You are less likely to repeat behaviors that don't bring positive results. In this way, you build up a repertoire of behaviors that to your mind are effective in eliciting the approval you need from your mother in order to feel worthwhile.

As long as you are able to elicit positive feedback from your mother and then by extension, from others around you, you are able to feel good about yourself, to feel worthwhile. In feeling good about yourself—good enough to have others value you—you may feel self-confident and appear to have positive self-esteem. Your view, as you experience yourself, is that you are worthy. You could be considered a high self-esteemer.

This is the situation with most of us for much or most of our lives. Because most mothers are attentive and affirming, most children, in their three-year-old narcissistic eyes, succeed at making them affirm them,. So most of us emerge from this time in our lives with the ability and confidence (in varying measures) to make our mothers and others value us. We emerge with a sense of what we call positive self-esteem, and we retain that as long as we are able to continue ensuring that others value us. With luck, this continues throughout our lifetime.

SUCCESSFUL LOW SELF-ESTEEM

This state, where you succeed at making others value you so that you feel worthwhile, is typically regarded as a state of positive self-esteem; I tend to think of it rather as a state of successful low self-esteem. In other words, you have succeeded in engaging others to counter your intrinsic low self-esteem, and, as a result, you feel worthwhile and continue to feel worthwhile for as long as others continue to validate you. Beneath your positive self-esteem lies your deeper and primal appreciation of your own intrinsic worth-lessness. Insofar as you are able to make others validate you, you can experience positive self-worth, but remember that this is grafted on top of your underlying low self-esteem. Therefore, successful low self-esteem seems a more accurate description of this state than positive self-esteem.

People differ in their ability to make others value them, and some are better than others at it. The more you succeed at having others value you, the more confident you are in your ability to make others value you, and the more confident about yourself you are. The opposite is equally true, in that the less successful you are at making others value you, the less self confident you are, and the less secure you are about your ability to make others value you.

Even the most outwardly confident and apparently successful people will likely experience low self-esteem if and when the conditions for external validation break down. We all aspire to the state of successful low self-esteem—that is, finding ways of being that ensure that others continue to validate us. Successful low self-esteem is and feels good and as long as you keep experiencing it, you will not feel the need to change anything in your life or your way of being.

I will discuss later how this state of successful low self-esteem can break down, what happens and how to deal with it when it does.

In A Nutshell

- You narcissistically misunderstand that unless you make your mother care for you, she won't, so you are compelled to make her care for you

- You narcissistically misunderstand that being cared for means that are worth being cared for

- The best way to make your mother care for you is by pleasing her

- Successfully pleasing her means you are worth being cared for, you are lovable, you are worthwhile. This is successful low self-esteem, and it feels good

CHAPTER 6

FROM PLEASING TO PERSONALITY: CREATING YOUR PERSONALITY

"Our humanity rests upon a series of learned behaviors, woven together into patterns that are infinitely fragile and never directly inherited."

— *Margaret Mead*

You may notice that your mother is cheerful and engages warmly when you smile, so you learn to smile more and more to keep her interest in you. You may notice that when you are distressed or in pain, she behaves very lovingly toward you. As a result, you learn to be fragile to keep her positive attention coming your way. You may experience her as withdrawn, and if you are cheerful and make her laugh, she emerges from her shell and pays you positive attention.

Being well behaved is a classic way to solicit her positive attention. You notice a connection between you behaving compliantly and her being pleased, and you determine that as long as you are obedient, she will be pleased, or at least will not be upset. She reinforces your good behavior, so you repeat it and become a well-behaved, obedient, and cooperative pleaser.

You discover through trial and error a number of different ways to behave that positively influence your mother's behavior toward you such that you feel cared for by her. Finding ways to please your mother becomes the active means of achieving positive self-esteem, or more accurately, successful low self-esteem.

So you learn to please in whatever ways seem to work for you; by achieving, impressing, competing, complying, caring, by being perfect, undemanding, invisible or whatever strategies works best with your mother in your unique circumstances with her and your family. As long as these behaviors prove effective, you commit yourself to them and become the person who achieves, impresses, amuses, takes care of, complies, makes few demands, sacrifices, and so on—whichever behaviors have the effect of eliciting validation from your mother.

A combination of these patterns emerges, is reinforced in the emotional hothouse of your family, and then becomes established as your way of being. This pattern of behaviors becomes you, the person you are, or your personality, the you that you take out into the world as you engage with life inside and outside of your family. Your personality becomes correspondingly more complex as you adopt more and different effective ways of inducing others to value you. As you succeed at inducing others to value you, you feel more valuable and experience a growing sense of positive self-regard and emotional security. As you come to rely on your ability to induce others to value you, you may develop the sense that you have the power to make others value you, and so you come to feel more empowered in this way.

These ways of being are not just how you behave; it is your personality, it is who you become and therefore who you are. You become the nurturer, the high achiever, the doormat, the clown, the buffoon, the complier, or the perfectionist. You become the person that learns to successfully please in the ways that work and that you reinforce by repetition. This becomes your true self.

And it is interesting to note from this perspective, that the person you become and the personality you develop is something that you determine, or have a large influence over. Personality is not simply thrust upon you, it does not emerge passively; rather, you exert a major influence over your personality, over who you decide to become under the overarching influence of the imperative to please your mother, and the other people upon whom you depend.

It is interesting how seldom people answer the question of who they are in terms of their personality style. People are more inclined to respond in terms of their social roles: they're a teacher, a mother, an uncle, a CEO, a professor, a daughter, a brother, and so on. People seldom think to answer the question of who they are in terms of the ways they please others or get their emotional needs met, of who they need to be or who they think they need to be to have their needs met. People seldom describe—let alone introduce themselves as the perfectionist, an entertainer, a self-effacing caregiver, or an ambitious, driven overachiever they learned to be. People generally are not very cognizant of the relationship between their learned ways of pleasing and their core identities, which is one of the reasons people find it so difficult to regain a healthy sense of themselves when their old ways of successfully eliciting positive regard from others stop working.

The following stories are about two of the people I have worked with who became who they are by taking on ways of being to elicit positive self-esteem from others to compensate for their innate sense of worthlessness.

SHEILA'S PERFECT LIFE

Sheila was in her early forties and had been depressed for years. Many different antidepressants and antidepressant combinations had afforded her brief respite from her symptoms, but she remained despondent, lethargic, exhausted and intensely self-loathing. She had been unable to work for a number of years and was eventually barely able to care of her teenage sons or do the housework. She was plagued by fits of extreme despair in which she had vivid images of killing herself by driving her car off the side of the road or into oncoming traffic. Sheila did not want to die and was not actively suicidal; she loved her husband and children deeply and did not want to do anything to hurt them but despite that, she was overcome by these profound moments of despair when all she could think of was dying. She was afraid that one day she might lose control and harm herself.

The treatments that had helped alleviate some of her other symptoms in the past had alleviated this most disturbing and alarming of symptoms. She had seen a therapist on and off over the years and found it helpful as long as she continued seeing the therapist. But the benefits faded as soon as she stopped the therapy.

Both she and her husband were worried, and frightened of what lay ahead for her. More medications were suggested, as was the prospect of electro-convulsive therapy (ECT). She was receptive to all suggestions, but skeptical that anything else would help, given her long history of only marginal and short-lasting benefits from the many previous treatments. Her specific questions to me were whether she had bipolar disorder, whether ECT would help her, and whether she would ever recover.

Sheila was a nurse and had been exceptionally competent and hardworking before the depression. She had risen rapidly through the ranks of her profession and eventually held a position of high responsibility. She was loved and admired by her colleagues, employers, and patients alike. She attained a fine balance between managing her marriage, her family, and her career. Her marriage was rock solid, and she and her husband were financially secure. She came from a large and close family and had five brothers and sisters, who all lived nearby. She had a large circle of friends, many of whom she'd had from her school days. She enjoyed a rich social life and was a gracious and generous hostess who created a warm atmosphere in her home. She always had an ear for other people's problems.

Everyone was shocked when she became unwell, and no one— least of all Sheila—could understand it. Her life was so full and stable; she seemed to have it all. Her collapse made no sense.

During therapy, she spoke of a normal childhood that was free of any trauma or abuse. But she described her mother as a self-involved woman who didn't seem to have much time for her children. She was demanding and somewhat controlling of Sheila and her siblings and only mildly encouraging. Sheila's sense was that when push came to shove, her mother didn't really care all that much about her or her siblings. She saw her mother as emotionally distant, a view that was shared by at least one of her sisters. She felt that she was never good enough for her mother—never good enough to command her interest and attention. Her father was a more generous emotional presence, but he was often away at work.

For as long as she could remember, Sheila had been a perfectionist. Everything had to be just so; otherwise she was ill at ease. She ran her house like the operating theater in the hospital: everything had to be in its right place and had to be so clean as to be almost sterile. She spent countless hours cleaning her home, scrubbing her bathtub so vigorously that she eventually scrubbed away the bathtub enamel. When her husband and children left the house in the morning, she would begin cleaning and would spend hours essentially sterilizing her home. This behavior increased over the years, especially after she stopped working, and she found it increasingly disconcerting and exhausting.

Sheila could not tolerate untidiness of any kind and kept getting into arguments with her children about the state of their rooms. She knew she was being unreasonable and was compromising her relationships with them, but she felt unable to stop herself. She was extremely invested in the impression her children made on others and became alarmed when one of them began to dress in an outlandish style.

She disclosed that she was a long-term secret binge eater and was disturbed at the steady increase in her weight. In front of her family she ate modestly, but she gorged herself when alone and would then purge. She was ashamed of this behavior, as she was with her compulsive cleaning. These behaviors had been present since her teens, but she had managed to keep them under control until the onset of her depression. She was never able to identify any particular trigger for her depression.

Sheila said that for as long as she could remember, her self-esteem had been low. But as long as she was able to keep things looking good, which for her meant looking perfect, she could feel okay about herself. She had no recollection of deciding to become a perfectionist or a high-achieving nurturer, and she had no idea why she needed to be liked and admired by others.

Sheila eventually came to understand through the therapy the connections between never feeling good enough, never feeling good enough for her mother and her strategies to remedy that. She realized that her efforts to be perfect were her ways of trying to induce her mother and then others to value her. She came to admit that she felt she could never afford to relax for fear of being ignored, which would lead to a withholding and withdrawal of affirmation, which in turn would force her to face her inner worthlessness. She came to appreciate how she came to these conclusions about herself on her own and that no one had ever done anything to her to make her feel bad about herself. She came to appreciate how she was the one who had established her ways of being—a perfect daughter, sister, student, nurse, manager, homemaker, wife, mother, friend—to ensure a steady external supply of self worth.

Sheila had always attributed her low self-esteem to her mother's lack of warmth and affection, but she was confused by her inability to offset that with the experience of all the love and devotion she enjoyed from so many different sources in her adult life. As she began to understand the workings of her cognitive narcissism, she was able to appreciate that her mother's self-absorption was not about her lack of worth but was simply the way her mother was. She gradually came to appreciate that her mother's way of being was not about her (Sheila) and had nothing to do with her.

These discoveries allowed Sheila to free herself from the compulsion to be perfect and from many of the self-soothing behaviors that accompanied her constant striving for perfection. She found herself increasingly free to adopt new and different ways of being, both with herself and in her relationships, ways of being that were less stressful and more satisfying.

Sheila's story illustrates how people learn to behave in order to secure the approval they need from others, the great lengths to which they go to receive a steady supply of validation, and the huge emotional price they sometimes pay in trying to ensure that validation keeps coming. Her story also highlights the false premises on which our conviction of our worthlessness rests and how awareness of them can start to set us free from the burdens of failed and failing low self-esteem.

BOB DOESN'T FIT IN

Bob was referred to the clinic after an unsuccessful suicide attempt that landed him in the hospital. He was in his mid-forties, married with three children, and had lived a cautious and unadventurous life. He was an accountant and a partner in an investment firm. He became depressed after an unwise investment failed and he lost a lot of money for both himself and his firm. But since he had followed company procedures in this investment, his firm had no quarrel with him over the matter. For his side, he'd had reservations about the investment, but went ahead anyhow in order to look good to his colleagues.

Bob experienced a profound loss of face over the fate of this failed investment. He felt that he was stupid, inept, and incompetent. He berated himself continually, ruminated on past failures, and viciously disparaged himself and his abilities. He felt diminished and could not sleep, eat, or concentrate. He could not face going into the office and seeing his colleagues, even though he knew that they did not blame him for the bad investment. Bob eventually stopped going to work and confined himself to his home. Then he became afraid that his wife would tire of him, especially after disclosing to her that he had made other unwise investments with their joint funds without consulting her.

Bob felt like an outsider at his firm, even though he had been a successful partner for several years. It was always a trial for him to sit through business meetings with his colleagues because, in his private thoughts, he felt that he did not deserve to be there and did not belong among them. He never felt good enough to be in their company (in both senses of the word). He felt he was constantly on the verge of being exposed as an ignoramus and a pretender. To protect himself from the rejection he imagined would follow any input he offered, he said very little in meetings. There were times when he felt he was doing well at work and was on top of particular projects, and at those times he felt more self-confident around his colleagues. But whenever he felt even a little out of his depth, his mind flooded with thoughts of inadequacy, exposure and imminent rejection.

In his depression Bob viewed his life as a constant stream of failures and his successes were hidden from his view. He became weepy at the drop of a hat, and this embarrassed him. He could not bear to be around people. In the incubator of his self-disparaging thoughts, he built up his ordinary shortcomings into monstrous failures. Life became unbearable, and he developed fantasies of being dead. He eventually decided to end his life and took the overdose of antidepressants and tranquilizers that landed him in the hospital. He felt like even more of a failure for having failed to end his life.

During therapy, Bob talked about growing up in a family where he was the middle of three sons. He described his family as normal and his as childhood as free from difficulties and traumas. Home life was calm and stable. He was well cared for and never lacked for anything. He had no complaints about his parents or his childhood.

He had the impression, however, that his father favored his older brother. His father and older brother spent a lot of time together, talking and fishing and playing ball. Bob felt excluded, that he didn't fit in, and he kept his distance. Meanwhile, his mother encouraged him in his schoolwork. He remembered deciding in elementary school that he would do well academically and he became determined to be the first university graduate and professional in his family. He succeeded on both counts.

Contrary to his expectations he found that being a university graduate and a professional didn't alter his sense of not fitting in, of not deserving to be part of an intimate circle. He continued to feel like an outsider and that he didn't fit in with his wife and his children, colleagues, or friends similar to how he had felt in his original family. He worked hard to try and fit in and earn his right to belong. But even so he always felt in his heart of hearts that he wasn't deserving, that he didn't really belong, and that even if he was welcomed into the inner circle, sooner or later others would discover that he was an imposter. The pressure to keep trying to earn his place in the inner sanctum and the accompanying expectation that at any moment he would be exposed became debilitating. The investment failure exacerbated these fears. In this highly agitated state of mind, he felt so worthless that life itself became unbearable, and in this frame of mind he attempted to end his life.

Bob came to understand how his view of himself as being worthless had come about as a result of his narcissistic interpretation of his unmet needs rather than because of his later sense of being excluded from the closeness between his father and older brother. He came to appreciate how his response to his conviction of his inadequacy inspired him to achieve academically and then professionally as a way of finding favor and fitting in.

Bob's story shows how we form our way of being in the world— in his case, by working very hard, even at times sabotaging himself (making an investment he has reservations about), just to be accepted (as someone who 'mans up' and makes investments). His story shows how we shape ourselves into people who try to extract validation from others by whatever means possible, how this can become unreliable and unstable, and what happens to us when it stops working. When it does, you encounter your inner worthlessness head on and develop the depressive and anxious symptoms that are the natural emotional accompaniments of worthlessness and low self-esteem.

Both Bob and Sheila show how we find explanations for the ways we are by referring to experiences in our childhood that we can remember, the self-absorbed mother in Sheila's case, the excluding father-brother bond in Bob's, how the explanations we come to become our stories, and how this overlooks the earlier factors that determine our inner sense of worthlessness, factors that we cannot remember or know about.

Bob and Sheila, like the rest of us, became the people they were in response to the beliefs they developed about their inherent lack of worth. These beliefs led them to find ways to ensure that they received the attention and validation they needed, first from their mothers and then from others. This external affirmation conveyed to them that they were worth caring about, that they were worth being kept alive. In their developing cognitively narcissistic minds, when they experienced care and being cared for, they understood that they were worth caring about and being kept alive. They understood that in order to receive care, it was up to them to make others care for them that they did by successfully pleasing others. They tried different ways of pleasing and formed their personalities around the results of their trial-and-error experiments of what was and wasn't pleasing to those they depended on. They became the people they thought they needed to be to secure a steady supply of validation and affirmation from their mothers.

As they continued to grow, they refined and adapted these affirmation-inducing strategies and applied them to the expanding world of other people upon whom their safety and well-being came to depend. Where able, they modified their ways of being to take account of the changing realities of their interactions with the increasingly diverse world of other people. Based on who they thought they needed to be to ensure that others would approve of them, they ultimately become the people they were by consolidating all the different effective ways they had discovered to make others affirm their worth.

These specific ways of being are what we refer to as personality, and this is how Sheila and Bob formed their personalities. This is as true for everyone as it was for them. We all follow the same process in learning to construct our own unique personalities—our distinct ways of being—behaving, reacting, and doing what we think we have to do to ensure that our needs are met and that we survive.

THE WORLD BEYOND YOUR MOTHER

The world beyond your mother is, of course, different in many ways from the conditions and circumstances of the formative stages of your relationship with her. How you learned to be may have been effective with your mother—that is, made her care for and attend to you—but may not work in other relationships and will certainly not work in all of your other relationships. The ways you learn to be when you are three will not necessarily ensure that people other than your mother will relate to you as though you were worth their while or worthwhile. Your father is likely to be influenced by different behaviors than your mother, as are your other caregivers, your brothers and sisters, your extended family members, and eventually your peers, friends, babysitters, classmates, teachers, colleagues, coworkers, neighbors, and anyone else you come into contact with as your world expands.

You learn to adapt what you have learned with your mother to fit your new and changing circumstances and expectations. You modify and refine some of your ways of being and may reserve certain behaviors for some situations and others for different situations. As you learn to navigate the world of ever-increasing emotional and interpersonal complexity, you learn additional ways to elicit affirming responses from others in order to feel and be worthwhile. As your repertoire of these ways of being expands, so do the ways in which you are able to make others think well of you and you habituate to doing what you can to look good to others, to putting on your best face or putting your best foot forward.

Although an infinite number of strategies are used to make others like and affirm you, it can be said that there are essentially two ways: induction and coercion.

Inducing others to approve of you is achieved by finding ways to please: by being obedient, cooperative, amusing, entertaining, beguiling, pretty, sexy, caring, solicitous, nurturing, competent, hardworking, productive, industrious, high achieving, undemanding, and so on. You may later use overt seduction and sex to make others approve of you. You may be genuine or pretend to be what you represent in order to have others like or affirm you. You may present yourself as someone who you think will appeal to others merely for the sake of appealing to others, even if it costs you emotionally or otherwise. You may feel compelled to behave in certain ways that you know are not right, or not right for you, but you do so to satisfy the more urgent need of securing someone else's validation. In all our personalities there is room for contradictions and incompatibilities, reflecting the differing and sometimes contradictory means of securing external supplies of self-worth from different sources.

Bob was haunted by the idea that his colleagues would "see through" him, that they would see that what he appeared to be— clever, reliable, bold and competent — was not the real Bob and that they would discover that the true Bob—the way he saw himself—was weak, ignorant, incapable, and needy. Bob saw himself as a pretender whose attempts to induce others to value him would eventually fail. His depression was both the result and proof of his failure. This idea of being seen through is not at all uncommon, and people can invest enormous amounts of effort into putting on and keeping up a front, with the underlying fear that one day it will come crashing down and they will be revealed as they truly are—or more accurately, as they see themselves—as essentially unworthy and dispensable.

The same is true for Sheila, who induced others to approve of her by appearing to be perfect. She believed that if she revealed any marks or blemishes—literally or figuratively—others would immediately see her as she saw herself: damaged, not good enough, and not worth caring about. She lived with the certainty and terror that her true self would eventually be exposed.

In A Nutshell

- You are narcissistically compelled to please your mother, and others, in order to be cared for, be loved, be worthwhile

- By trial and error you find different ways to be and behave that successfully please your mother and others

- You become the person who learns to successfully please in the ways that work for you

- In this way you construct your personality

CHAPTER 7

COERCION: THE ALTERNATIVE TO PLEASING

"War is like love, it always finds a way."

— *Bertold Brecht*

Since most mothers care for their children, and since most children are cared for, most children find ways to successfully please their mothers. Bu this is not always the case. Not everyone is able to suffi-ciently please their mothers (or others). For a variety of reasons, not all mothers are easily pleased, or pleased at all, at least not from the child's point of view. What is required to please successfully may not be possible for a child, and some children may be unable to find ways to please their mothers or others on whom they depend.

When pleasing is not an option, the alternative is coercion or the use of force. You may direct force in one of two directions, either inwardly against your self or outwardly towards others. You direct force against yourself by attacking yourself and making yourself injured or unwell and behave in a sickly, passive, needy, complaining or naggy way. You may direct force inwardly against yourself by claiming to be in pain or ill in an effort to force your mother to attend to you. In this way you are attacking yourself, making yourself unwell in order to attract your mother's attention that you feel you wouldn't otherwise receive.

If this becomes your primary means of making others attend to and validate you, you may grow up to be hypochondriachal, in other words, someone who worries about and complains of various ailments to receive sympathy and attention. People like this feel unable to attract sufficient attention when they're well and healthy, but when they're unwell, then others such as their partners, their family, friends, colleagues, doctors, and nurses and other medical staff attend to them and validate them in ways they would not otherwise receive. So this kind of hypochondriasis for the benefit of gaining your mother's and later others' sympathy, attention and care is a way of using force against yourself when pleasing fails.

In Aesop's fable *The Boy Who Cried Wolf*, a bored shepherd amuses himself by crying wolf to alarm the villagers. He is killed by a real wolf when the villagers, after having been duped one too many times, do not believe him when one day a wolf really does confront him. The shepherd had learned to draw attention to himself on the false grounds that something was the matter. This is not dissimilar from the situation of the hypochondriachal person who complains of nonexistent symptoms or ailments to receive attention.

Force can also be directed outwardly, towards your mother or other people or toward things. You may hit and hurt your mother and others or be destructive towards objects as a way of making your mother attend to you when you are unable to gain her attention in more constructive ways. Displeasing her becomes an option when pleasing her fails because at least she focuses on you. Negative attention is better than no attention at all.

When the outward use and threat of force becomes your primary means of inducing others to validate and affirm you, you become a bully. You may threaten to beat up other kids at school if they don't voluntarily affirm you and show you that they regard you well. You use force to make them give you something of value that symbolizes worth that they would not give you freely. You grow up to be a bully or a thug, using force and violence to get others to value you by forcibly taking from them tokens of value that they would not otherwise or freely give you. Stealing is a great example of this sort of outwardly directed use of force to gain something of value from someone who wouldn't freely grant it to you. The preoccupation of some teenagers and gangsters with being "dissed," or disrespected, and the threats of violence to enforce this respect come to mind as a more abstract expression of externally sourced coerced worth.

VIOLENT VINCE

Vince's parents were unable to nurture or encourage him. His father was a harsh, critical, and unloving man, even on the rare occasions he was sober. His sudden disappearance from the family when Vince was four solved some problems but created others. His mother was a fragile woman with little self-confidence and few marketable work skills, and she was unable to fill the economic and emotional vacuum left by her husband's disappearance. She became the sole breadwinner and worked hard to provide for her children. As a result of her work she was away from home much of the time, and when she was home, she was too exhausted to provide emotional support to her children.

Vince neither helped nor added to his mother's burdens. From an early age he was dejected and withdrawn. He became a loner; his friends were other loners and people who didn't fit in. He lost interest in his schoolwork and dropped out of school in ninth grade. He began selling drugs and stealing. He took an occasional job on a construction site but had no steady work. He left home and drifted. He remained a loner but found a girlfriend. The relationship was volatile and unstable, with neither Vince nor his girlfriend being able to provide love or support for the other.

The girlfriend became pregnant and decided she wanted the baby, even though she and Vince could not really provide for a child. Their relationship ended before their daughter was born, but Vince stayed in the picture because of the child. His relationship with his ex-girlfriend remained volatile, and they had frequent arguments about various aspects of child care and his failure to provide regular support payments. Vince enjoyed the role and the status of being a father but had little idea of the responsibilities and skills required for fatherhood. He continued to drift, to fight with his ex-girlfriend, and to see his daughter when he felt like it.

The event that brought Vince to the psychiatric ward was when he pulled a knife on his two-year-old daughter. He had become incensed after a row when his ex refused him contact with his daughter because of his irresponsibility. In a rage, he forced his way into their house and grabbed his daughter. He held a knife to her throat and threatened to hurt her unless his ex gave in to his demands. She called the police, and Vince landed up in the hospital.

While Vince had not intended to actually harm his daughter, his inability to have his way with his ex led him to this fit of rage and to this dramatic way of trying to force his ex to meet his needs. Though this was not the first time he had used force to get his way, it was the first time his use of force had threatened his child.

During our discussions in the hospital, Vince blamed his ex for provoking him and later blamed his parents and a host of other people who, in his mind, had let him down in one way or another throughout his life. Coercion and aggression were his primary strategies for having his needs met, and this had been the case for as long as he could remember. He had no idea what it meant to be responsible for his actions; instead, he blamed others for not giving him what he wanted and for not meeting his needs. Even in the face of such catastrophic behavior toward his daughter, he could not get beyond blaming others for his problems.

Vince came to understand the limitations of violence as a means of eliciting external validation, yet he remained closed to the possibility of learning more effective and acceptable ways of interacting with others to have his needs met. He left the hospital as bitter and self-righteous as he was when he entered it and as ill equipped to take care of either his daughter or himself as before.

Coercive attention-seeking behaviours are ways of forcing others to pay you attention when your ability to induce them to validate you is ineffective. Inducing or pleasing behavior is, in this sense, no less attention seeking than the negative, destructive, and self-destructive behaviors - the difference is that coercive behaviours tend to be destructive and maladaptive, whereas pleasing behaviours tend to be constructive and adaptive.

RACHEL GETTING MARRIED: DIFFERENT WAYS TO GET YOUR NEEDS MET

The 2008 film *Rachel Getting Married* speaks eloquently to these two alternative modes of engaging your mother and others in the unending quest of extracting confirmation of your worth from others. As Rachel (played by Rosemarie DeWitt) is preparing for her wedding, her younger sister, Kym (Anne Hathaway), returns home for the wedding from a drug rehabilitation center. The drama revolves, excruciatingly and at times hilariously, around the ghosts that emerge from the family closet, principally between Kym and her mother, Abby (Debra Winger). Abby has always been an ineffectual, self-absorbed, and immature woman incapable of adequately parenting her children. Both daughters deal with their experience of inadequate mothering—and in turn the difficulties of reliably extracting affirmation from their mother—differently.

Rachel goes the pleasing route, becoming a nurturing, thoughtful, considerate person who epitomizes these adaptive choices in becoming a therapist. Kym chooses the coercive path, becoming destructive and self-destructive in the process. She seems as set on her unremitting course of coercion as Rachel is on her relentless path of pleasing. The film beautifully resolves these dynamics in the denouement when Abby excuses herself—inexcusably—from the wedding post mortem with her daughters. At that moment the sisters look across the expanse of their emotionally vacuous mother at each other and share the same realization: that their understanding of their lack of worth has been a misinterpretation of their mother's failure to affirm them - their mother's failure to sufficiently validate and affirm them has not been due to their perceived unlovability, but is instead due to her own self-absorption and insecurities that have nothing to do with the daughters. This realization sets the daughters instantly free (remember, it's fiction), and the film captures their unspoken epiphanies and emergent freedoms sensitively and exquisitely.

People learn many different ways of behaving to try to make others care for them and there is an almost infinite variety of different ways to make others validate and affirm us. Many are constructive and positive, but others are counterproductive, destructive, and self-destructive. These different ways of behaving, and the unique ways they come together in each individual, consolidate to form personality. The many different ways of inducing and coercing others to validate and affirm you reflect the many different types of personality that exist. In this sense, all behavior is attention-seeking, the constructive and adaptive pleasing behaviours no less than the negative, destructive, and self-destructive behaviors that we commonly think of as attention seeking. The differences between these different ways of getting others to affirm and validate you—is not so much whether they are attention seeking or not, but more in how productive or counterproductive they are.

YOUR CHANGING AUDIENCE

As you grow during childhood, so does your capacity for earning regard and approval from others. You become more dexterous and better informed, and you are presented with new arenas where you can do well, thrive, and prosper, and so earn the esteem of others. You grow taller and stronger. You learn to dress and bathe yourself. You learn to groom yourself and are able to do more chores around the house. You learn to do things like run, swim, skip, ride a bicycle. You attend school and learn things about the world. You are tested on your learning abilities, and as you master more and more actions and functions, and acquire more knowledge, you are able to earn more positive regard for your expanding repertoire of abilities and performances.

In these early years, you depend on your parents and other people older than you to secure your survival. You simply don't have the wherewithal to take care of yourself to ensure your physical survival on your own. This means that the audience you most need to care for you, and to please is your parents and other adults. Without their care and protection, your chances of surviving to adulthood are diminished. This is as true today as it was in times past. Therefore, the audience you need to make care for you is the adults immediately around you.

As you reach your teens, your reliance on adults diminishes. You grow and become bigger, stronger, and smart enough to be able to rely on yourself and your own resources to survive from one day to the next. You don't need adults in the same way you did when you were small and vulnerable. From your early to middle teens onward, the others upon whom your survival depends shifts to an entirely different group, namely your peers. Your peers include potential mates as well as competitors for those potential mates.

If you think about this from the perspective of the gene—the part of all living matter that truly lives through time—all that is required for the gene to live is to make it from one generation to the next. In animals, humans included, (despite advances in cloning technology), this is accomplished through intercourse and reproduction. Conception, gestation, delivery, and childrearing are required to bring the gene into the next generation or phase of the gene's life. To get to the next life phase, that gene has to connect with genes carried by different gene carriers in order to create a new fetus that will be born and live—hopefully—to the stage where it too can reproduce itself and keep the genes it carries traveling forward in time, in life.

In this scheme, adults are needed for the creation of the being that you become and then for protecting that gene-carrying being until it is able to reproduce itself into the next generation of gene-carrying beings. Your parents are the adults with the biggest interest in protecting the gene-carrying being that is you. Each of us is our parents' genetic heritage, and we represent their best chance of having their genes continue on.

But when you no longer need your parents to keep you safe from threats to your survival and become biologically capable of reproduction yourself—when you enter your teens or adolescence —your dependence on your parents drops off as you can now better meet your survival needs on your own and so your need for their approval declines.

Your survival, as in the survival of the genes you carry, depends on you reproducing yourself, becoming a parent of children who will carry your genes on to the next generation. Your chances of achieving that reproduction no longer depend on your parents or the generation preceding you but rather on your own generation of peers, firstly in terms of securing a mate with whom to reproduce, and then in terms of being able to survive the competition for that mate. You will most likely be a link in the chain of your genes' lives, rather than the end of the road, to the extent that you can find a suitable (genetically speaking) mate and rear your offspring to the point where they can reproduce themselves. For most of human history your chances of achieving this was increased among potential mates of your own generation rather than those of an older generation. To this end, once you become a teen, your survival now depends more on your contemporaries than your parents and their generation.

Since you now need to be able to appeal to your peers and contemporaries more than to your parents and their generation, the qualities that appealed to your parents and their generation when you were younger may not be the same qualities that appeal to your contemporaries, the new audience on whom your survival now depends. Being physically attractive is likely not as important a quality to your parents as it is to your potential mates and competitors. Being studious is likely an important quality to your parents but may be less so for your peers. There is of course some overlap between qualities that appeal to both audiences; it would be biologically inefficient if there were no overlap at all. Once you leave childhood behind, you require new ways of being—modifications to your ways of being— that will succeed in making your new audience of positive-esteem providers come through for you and give you the affirmation you need to feel worthwhile.

Teenagers go to great lengths to make themselves attractive to their new audience of peers. Who can forget the lengths to which we went to achieve that, the many hours spent in front of the mirror, scrutinizing every aspect of our appearance in minute detail? We were exquisitely self-conscious of our looks and sensitive to what others thought of them. Many of us never get over this sensitivity about our appearance as a measure of our desirability, and therefore our intrinsic worth. We go to great lengths to improve our physical appearance and are happily helped along the industries that are devoted to giving us an edge over the competition. Beauty and hair salons, spas and wellness centers, fashion houses, gyms and sports clubs, advertising and the mass media, and plastic and cosmetic surgery and dentistry are just some of the industries that reinforce our reliance on good looks and a favorable physique as a way of eliciting approval from others, this being the way we measure our worth (or lack thereof).

The point is that once you become a young adult and no longer need your parents and other adults to ensure your survival and well-being, you change your ways of earning the affirmation and esteem you still require to please your peers, the new audience your continued survival and security depend on. To this end, you may give up on strategies that worked before but no longer do with this new audience, and adopt new ways of being that more effectively secures you validation and esteem from your new audience of peers.

THE UGLY DUCKLING

The tale of the ugly duckling speaks to this theme of being unable to please your original group and then at adolescence, finding a new group that you are able to please. The ugly duckling is born into an environment where he looks so different from all the other ducklings, he doesn't fit in and can't win the approval of the others. His survival is at stake because of his inability to induce others to appreciate him. His childhood is a litany of rejection and dread of abandonment and death. There is nothing he can do to make anyone value him and he becomes self-loathing and depressed. Then along comes adolescence, and the duckling morphs into a swan and becomes his undeniably beautiful self, joins up with other swans that readily accept him, and, for the first time in his life, fits in and is happy. As he becomes an adult, he becomes different from how he was before, he changes and successfully appeals to a new audience that accepts him and affirms his self worth.

The ugly duckling represents the dream that many people with unsuccessful low self-esteem harbor: that they will turn into something beautiful and be discovered and desired by all and live happily ever after. The miraculous and fairy tale context of this theme invariably means that the previously unhappy character meets someone who values and validates him or her for the rest of their life. This speaks to the notion that personality changes and remains fluid allowing you the possibility of modifying your repertoire of behaviors to increase your chances of inducing a new audience to value you.

We all cultivate our own ways of being to fit our circumstances, from the earliest parts of our lives and on an ongoing basis as the need requires and our capacity to change allows. There is a wide range of different ways of being to attract and maintain the approval of others, and these different ways of being are reflected in the multitude of different personalities and personality styles. While there is some truth to the idea that personality becomes fixed by early adulthood, there remains the possibility of change and adaptation, even in the later years of one's life.

It is important to note that this way of becoming yourself is natural, and that there is nothing wrong or pathological about it. Via these dynamics you become who you are and do what you do, always emotionally governed by the need to look good and be attractive to others or at least to certain select others. Whatever you do, you do it to look good to someone whose opinion you hold in high regard.

In A Nutshell

- If pleasing fails to sufficiently make others meet your needs, your next best option is to use force

- Force can be directed against yourself (the source of hypochondriasis, drug abuse and other self destructive behaviours) or against others (the source of bullying and criminality)

- Adolescence requires you to rely on peers rather than parents to meet your survival needs. This may require a change of strategies to have your needs met

---

CHAPTER 8

WHEN PLEASING FAILS

"Humanity i love you because / when you're hard up you pawn your / intelligence to buy a drink."

— *e. e. cummings, "Humanity i love you"*

You can build a wonderful world for yourself on the basis of who you make yourself become. Because the things that please your mother are generally the things that please others in your community, you learn to please the world at large as you do things that please and benefit others. You persist in these ways of being for as long as they hold up and secure you the affirmation you seek. You are able to make adjustments to meet changed circumstances. And as long as the world cooperates with the arrangement of providing you with self-worth as long as you continue to please, and make the small adjustments required to continue pleasing, you are hypothetically able to maintain your way of being and your accompanying contentment for as long as you live.

If you are really lucky you will go to your grave with that arrangement intact, your strategies for gaining the approval of the world effective, and yourself full of positive self-regard. We all know people like this—or whom we think are like this—people who seem to be and whom we think of as self-confident, secure, and full of high self-esteem. You think you are the only one who struggles with self-esteem issues, without realizing that everybody, to a greater or lesser extent, struggles with the same issues. The idea that it is only you who struggles with self-esteem and that everyone else is secure and confident is in itself an interesting manifestation of cognitive narcissism.

What is far more likely than this scenario of your ways of successfully inducing the world to value you lasting your whole lifetime, is that somewhere along the way, sooner or later, the successful ways of being that you originally mastered begin to fail you.

When this happens, it is a challenge to work out an alternative way to be and to restore the status quo where the world will validate you once more. Sheila cleaned more and more vigorously as she felt less and less return from her established ways of eliciting self-esteem, fruitlessly scrubbing the bathtub until the enamel began to wear off. She felt compelled to do work harder at the strategies she thought had worked before. The increased scrubbing brought her a diminishing sense of value, to the point where she saw it as futile and ridiculous. But she did not know how to stop. Her first instinct was to simply work harder, to put even more effort into the strategy that had been effective before. When this strategy failed to bring her the sense of worth she craved, she began to numb herself and her feelings of despair and worthlessness with food. This led to the vicious cycle in which she felt even worse about herself for her binge eating and her inability to lose the weight she gained. This cycle led to her feeling irredeemably bad about herself. She did not know how to make others validate her anymore, and she became increasingly desperate and depressed.

Phil experienced similar difficulties when his ways of feeling good about himself failed after he was unable to resolve conflicts among his office staff. He was accustomed to feeling highly effective in everything he did and believed his inability to ease the tensions in his office was a sign of his fallibility. He feared others would see through his façade of competence and see him as he saw himself: as an incompetent and undeserving person who had to impress others with his achievements in order to feel worthwhile. In failing to deal adequately with his office situation, he thought that his weaknesses were exposed for all to see and he despaired of being able to earn back the high regard he previously commanded from others.

Anxious about being discovered as worthless, Phil slipped into a state of depression. He became afraid to go out in public because he thought his inadequacies were transparent, clearly visible for everyone to see. He did not know how to manage his fears, and his shame over the labels "depression" and "anxiety" compounded his convictions of his intrinsic worthlessness. He remained incapacitated despite psychiatric medication and was unable to go to work and face his staff. He was stuck and did not know how to get unstuck.

This is what can happen when the old ways of being and of inducing others to value you stop working: you get stuck in your old ways and don't know how to get unstuck. This very unpleasant state is frequently called depression and regarded as a sickness, but can equally be seen as a state of emotional stuckness.

It seems that this state occurs with growing frequency in our time and in our society. Depression is recognized as a major public health problem and anti-depressants are the second most commonly pre-scribed group of medications in the United States of America (after lipid regulators).

WHY PLEASING FAILS

Let us consider why the strategies you establish early in your life so often seem to stop working and the arrangement you have with the world to validate you breaks down so often?

I will consider just two of the many reasons why the world gives up on validating you.

In the first instance, you may live too long. Let's speculate that the arrangement where you behave in ways that please others and that in turn, others validate you, first fell into place a long time ago, many thousands of years ago. Back then, people did not live as long as they do now. Even a hundred years ago, most people even in North America had a life expectancy in their mid- to late forties. Today the average North American can expect to live into their early or even late-eighties. People nowadays live almost twice as long as they did a hundred years ago, and maybe even as much as three times longer than in earlier times in history, not to mention prehistory.

So, this mutually pleasing arrangement that originally was expected to last thirty or forty years must now last at least twice as long. If a machine is designed to last for ten years and is still in use after twenty years, chances are that it will break down. The reality of successful living that increases human longevity places this arrange-ment in jeopardy. As you get older, the likelihood that your reliance on others for your sense of self worth will break down and you will become depressed, increases.

Take the example of a person who earns their self-esteem by working and providing for their family. He or she learns a job, cultivates work habits, labors for several decades, and earns their self-worth from the employer in the form of salary, by which they feed their family and from whom they then earn more positive esteem. If this person dies at forty-five while still employed, he or she will go to their grave with this arrangement for pleasing and affirmation, for successful low self-esteem, still intact.

In todays world, however, it is likely this person will still be living at sixty-five, perhaps even at eighty-five. At the age of forty-five or fifty-five, they may find themselves replaced by a cheaper or better employee. And at a later age they will likely find themselves retired, possibly with another twenty years of life still ahead of them. They still know how to earn a salary and self-esteem from the world, but after retirement, the world no longer provides it. While he or she sticks to their end of the bargain, the world reneges.

The point is that something that was designed to last for thirty, forty, or fifty years cannot reasonably be expected to still be working ten, twenty, or thirty years later, at least not with the same efficiency and not without breaking down and needing repairs. In this way human longevity is a cause for the collapse of the arrangement whereby you earn your self-esteem from the world. The dumb and blind force of successful living and ageing undermines the mutually satisfying arrangement where you please the world and the world affirms and values you.

Another reason this arrangement breaks down is the changing nature of the world. Chances are that the world you were born into is not the same world that you inhabit now. In the old days, and for most of human history, most people lived in pretty much the same circumstances they were born into. They lived among the same few hundred or thousand people in the same village all their lives, and they probably died without traveling beyond a ten-mile radius of where they were born. The people they grew up with were the same people they spent their adult lives with. Their activities, rituals, and traditions remained the same from one year to the next, from one generation to the next. Nothing changed much in their daily routines or in their experience of the world.

In other words, the ways people learned to earn approval from the world when they were young continued to work through their later lives because their world—the conditions and circumstances of their lives—remained constant.

But when the situation changes, then the strategies that were crafted specifically for circumstances that have changed and become outdated will no longer work.

One generalization we can make about the modern world is that change is the new norm, and continuity and constancy are the exception, not the rule. Fewer people live in the rural communities anymore; more and more people live in sprawling metropolises. There is a big difference between living among the few hundred people you have known all your life and living among millions of strangers who know nothing about you and about whom you know little or nothing. You are less likely to earn positive self-regard from strangers than from people who have known you all your life since childhood. It is much more difficult to know how to please strangers and to keep pleasing a constantly changing cast of characters in the modern, overcrowded and anonymous world than it was in the small, predictable and unchanging world of former times.

In the most modern version of our contemporary world, in the technological, electronic or digital age we live in now, the rate of change keeps increasing. Things not only change, but change quickly, all the time and more and more rapidly. As a result, it becomes harder to keep up with the changes and the ways things are done when from one year to the next, they keep being done differently. The ways you make phone calls, listen to music, travel, play, purchase, pay and communicate changes with ever-increasing speed. What worked last year may not work this year or the next, and what was in last year is now likely passé.

The people you rub shoulders with every day, whether on public transport, in the street, at the supermarket, are anonymous and change from one day to the next. The people you work with are different from the people you knew when you were young and learning how to please. Expectations change, standards change, conditions change; you can't even be sure that your job will be the same from one year to the next.

In this modern world, you have more choices than ever before. If you don't like something, it is easier than ever to end your relationship with it, to walk away and start over with something else. Which means that from another perspective, it is just as easy for someone to lose interest in you and walk away from you. The modern world offers much more room for changes of heart, of mind, of activity, of location, of surroundings, of interest, and of relationship—than ever before in human history.

Imagine yourself as someone who earns your self-worth by nurturing, particularly by nurturing your children. In the past, you would raise your children and they would grow up and then raise their own families close to you, if not in the same house. This was the case for most of human history: your children and then your grand-children were always in close proximity to you. This means that as a nurturer, as someone who earns self-worth by nurturing others, you always had someone on hand to nurture. In the modern age, the chances that your grandchildren live in the same town, city, or even state or province as you are much lower, so as someone who earns self-worth principally by nurturing others, the opportunities for you to do so diminish, and the arrangement of you earning positive self-esteem by nurturing is undermined and breaks down.

Under conditions of constant change, the chances that the ways you learned to please when you were very young will still be working as effectively thirty, forty, or more years later becomes increasingly less likely. Sooner or later, your ways of pleasing will stop working because the world they were designed to work in has changed. The conditions under which you learned to please no longer exist, and your ways of successfully pleasing no longer fit the new conditions of your life.

For both these reasons—longevity and change—your ability to please is ever more likely to fall off and fail over time. When that happens, and you can no longer make others value you, you revert to your base state of worthlessness, which in today's world is identified as depression.

TRY, TRY, TRY AGAIN

Earning self-esteem is a never-ending quest. You have to work at it continually. It's almost as though you're only as good as your last performance. As soon as you stop performing, you run the risk of no more positive regard coming your way, and when that happens, you are faced with your inner conviction of your innate worthlessness. In fact, your low self-esteem is always just outside the door, waiting for a chance to come in and reassert itself. It is a monster you have to feed constantly to prevent it from feeding off you.

You become adept at recognizing when the monster is hungry—when your external supply of positive regard is running low—and responding quickly to the threat. The most natural and instinctive first response to this is to try harder at the very ways you know from experience have been effective in the past. If being industrious and achieving has been a successful way to ensure a steady supply of self-esteem in the past, it is likely to be effective again, so when you are threatened with losing external validation, you instinctively work and strive harder. If accumulating money or possessions has been effective before, you will likely endeavor to acquire more stuff. If being thin, looking good, or being a martyr has worked for you in the past, chances are that losing weight, having plastic surgery, or sacrificing yourself even more will work next time.

When you feel your sources and supplies of self-worth are threatened, you revert to your strategies that have been successful in the past. On the balance of probabilities, if it worked before, it is likely, though not guaranteed, to work again. This is how some people find themselves taking work home with them, staying later at the office, working weekends—working harder and harder to maintain their supply of self-esteem and ultimately becoming workaholics and becoming burnt out. You work harder and harder but get less and less in return, you exhaust yourself to no avail, because in spite of working harder, the supply of positive regard does not materialize.

This is similar to how some people get into the frantic pursuit and accumulation of wealth and power, yet remain emotionally empty, unnourished, and unhappy because as these symbols of worth lose their power to affirm and validate, you feel compelled to work harder to acquire more of them.

Trying harder in these ways is not a negative or bad thing, and is sometimes if not often a successful way to restore the connection between effort and the reward of earning self regard. If and when and for as long as it works, it is beneficial and adaptive. You are able to restore a source of self worth, and so experience yourself as being worthwhile, which feels good, you are happy and content, and that's the way things ought to be. You're back to successful low self-esteem.

TRYING SMARTER, NOT JUST HARDER

As long as your successful ways of pleasing hold up, you feel worthwhile. As long as what you have learned continues to fit your experiences, you can feel confident and secure in the knowledge of your ability to make the world value you. But if and when and for whatever reason you fail to elicit the affirming responses you need from others, and trying harder doesn't work, you will look for new and different ways to make others value you. You modify your behavior or give up a behavior that has become ineffectual.

If you cannot find any way to make person A supply you with positive self-worth, you may decide to find someone else instead and replace person A with person B. If it works, your sense of worth is restored and you're happy.

In the modern world you have more and more access to alternate ways to find external suppliers of your self worth. You can change partners more easily now than in most periods of human history, and it is increasingly easy to get a divorce and find a new partner. The internet makes it especially easy to find a new partner or new partners. Nowadays you can change your work, where you work, the people you work with and even the kind of work you do more easily than ever before. You can even change careers mid-way through or late in your life to find new ways of earning both a living and self-esteem. This was not possible before.

It is easier to change location and domicile than it was in the past and a plane ticket will get you to a new city or country or even a new continent in a matter of hours. If your looks start to fade, you get have them restored surgically now more easily than at any other time in history. You can start to exercise, and change your diet to make yourself not only healthier but also more physically attractive. You can take up all manner of new interests and activities to find new people and new ways to be validated and affirmed.

Psychotherapy and counseling are now available as ways to learn new strategies, alongside a host of other approaches that emphasize personal growth, personal empowerment, and related interventions. Drug rehabilitation, anger management, and assertiveness training are some additional ways to acquire new strategies of inducing others to validate you.

You can now not only work harder at the old ways of earning self-worth, but also smarter in terms of finding new ways to earn regard from others.

The folk tale "The Three Little Pigs" speaks to this idea of trying smarter, not just harder. As you may recall, the first pig builds a house of straw, which the wolf blows down. The second pig builds a house of wood that, while stronger than the first house, is also destroyed. The third pig builds a house of bricks, which is so strong the wolf cannot blow it down, no matter how much he huffs and puffs.

In this story the three pigs represent the steps someone goes through in trying harder and smarter to build self-worth and personal security through progressively greater and more studied effort. Since it is harder to build with wood than straw, and hardest of all to build with bricks, that building with bricks takes more time, effort and know how, the message is that the more effort you make, the more likely it is that you will be rewarded by the world around you and the more content and secure you will be.

People are inclined to behave as the little pigs did in trying to wolf-proof or disaster-proof their lives. Even though it is not always possible to switch seamlessly or effortlessly from one strategy to another, from one material circumstance to another, it is easier now than probably ever before in human history to switch from straw to wood and from wood to brick, from one strategy for securing affirmation from the world to another. In modern society, you have more and more opportunities to change your strategies for securing new sources of self-worth.

So the two main ways to restore your successful low self-esteem are trying harder and trying smarter. For as long as they work, you experience yourself as worthwhile and therefore feel content or happy.

EMOTIONAL ANESTHESIA

Once your strategies of maintaining and restoring successful low self-esteem fail, your self-esteem fails. Once that happens, you find yourself stuck in a situation where you no longer know how to make the outside world affirm you. And being without an outside source of positive self-worth, you revert to your original state of low self-worth. As shown by Humpty Dumpty, unmitigated worthlessness is overwhelming, unbearable, and catastrophic.

Feeling worthless means feeling not only that no one thinks well of you, but also that you are not sufficiently important enough to anyone that they should bother to keep you alive. Of course, once you are an adult—unlike when you were younger and dependent on others to keep you safe—it is no longer a matter of actual or physical life and death. You are able to see to your own basic survival needs; you don't depend on others in the same way as you did when you were three. But you still depend on others, in the sense that without others valuing you, you are worthless and dispensable; your existence counts for nothing and it is like a life-or-death situation. The feelings that accompany this state are intensely negative and emotionally painful. And when you are stuck with no other ways to change your conditions to dispel these feelings, the best you can then do is to find ways to dull or extinguish these despairing feelings.

The best way to do that is by numbing yourself.

And the easiest way to numb yourself is by putting something into your body, or to drug yourself.

For thousands of years, humans have used alcohol for a variety of reasons and purposes, including as a means of numbing their painful emotions, and inducing a state of emotional anesthesia. Over the course of time, humans have found naturally occurring substances and compounds, or drugs, to accomplish this. I once read an anthropological theory that mankind transitioned from hunter-gatherers to agriculturalists specifically to cultivate wheat because you make alcohol from grain. Who knows how true this is, but it is an interesting idea.

Drugs and alcohol are very effective ways to numb yourself to painful emotions in the short-term. Since the benefits are short-lived, when the effects wear off, you find yourself back in the same state of emotional pain you were in before and so you may need to take more of the same drug for another short-lived respite. If you keep up this pattern, you may become addicted to using drugs to numb yourself. As the addiction worsens, you may reach a point where the substances creates new problems and worsens your self-esteem affliction. Drugs and alcohol can become self-destructive if you come to rely on them as the primary or sole means to numb your pain and provide relief from the despair of worthlessness.

You may go to great lengths to acquire the drugs and you may lose sight of their harmful effects on you and on others around you. Yet despite of the hazards of drugs and alcohol, they remain common—if not the most common—remedies that people turn to when they are stuck not knowing how to get others to affirm and validate them and provide them with self-worth.

Prescription drugs may be used for similar purposes as recreational or street drugs and alcohol. Instead of going to the liquor store or a dealer, it is common and more acceptable to see a doctor for your emotional anesthetic. As a result, psychiatric medicines are very widely prescribed and used.

Antidepressants and tranquilizers perform the same function as alcohol and street drugs in the sense that they lessen your feelings of distress and numb you to the pain of feeling not good enough. They may even provide you with an artificial "high" or a feeling of well-being—a feeling of being important and worthwhile—although most prescription drugs have fewer of those effects than illicit drugs. Overall, today's prescription drugs are safer than alcohol and street drugs, but are often no more effective as emotional anesthetics than alcohol and recreational drugs.

This is not to say that these prescription medications do not have their uses; they are in fact vital in the treatment of psychiatric diseases and can have life saving benefits. But when used to mollify the increasingly common negative emotional states associated with self-esteem failure, they have no more value than cocaine or whiskey.

Alcohol, street drugs, and prescription medications can all effectively and temporarily alleviate unpleasant emotional states, but none of them can change the conditions that gave rise to these states in the first place.

DISTRACTION AND VICARIOUS LIVING

Not everyone has a taste for alcohol, street drugs, or medications, so some people find other ways to cope with the anguish of failed low self-esteem. Food can become a means of soothing yourself and achieving temporary relief from feelings of worthlessness, as can high risk activities like gambling, high-risk sports or promiscuous sex. You may distract yourself temporarily by living vicariously through reality TV shows and other media, entertainment and celebrity fixations. The contemporary world offers an endless array of means to distract us from the distress of failing low self-esteem. Some are healthier than others, but even the healthiest offer no more than distraction from the anguish of failing low self-worth.

In A Nutshell

- Your strategies to make others care for you may stop working when the conditions of your life and of the world around you change

- When this happens, you can try harder at what worked before, or you can try new strategies to make others value you

- When you cannot think of any other ways to make others value you, you get **stuck** in a place of 'failed low self-esteem' (in contrast to successful low self-esteem). This feels terrible

- Numbing your painful emotions with drugs or pills then becomes your best way to cope with failing low self-esteem

---

CHAPTER 9

STRESS AND THE ONSET OF SYMPTOMS

"An' for every hung-up person in the whole wide universe."

— *Bob Dylan*

When you reach the point where you can no longer tolerate the unbearable awareness of failed low self-esteem, you become stressed and develop symptoms of stress and distress. Stress has both physical and emotional features, and the common emotional manifestations are depression and anxiety.

Depression is experienced as a sense of sadness and misery. Your joy at pleasurable things declines, and fewer and fewer things please you until nothing pleases you anymore. You withdraw activities that were previously enjoyable including from company. You lose energy, become lethargic and you tire easily. Everything becomes an effort. Your sleep becomes disrupted and this may make you even more tired. You lose interest in things including food and you may start to lose weight.

You become preoccupied with your failings, your mistakes and mis-steps, and in your mind you magnify their significance. You beat up on yourself, blame yourself and feel excessively guilty. You fixate on your intrinsic lack of worth and feel worthless, hopeless and maybe even helpless. You shun company yet often feel terribly lonely. You can be irritable. You worry too much and unreasonably about even the smallest matters and may have actual anxiety attacks.

It seems as though nothing will ever improve. Your future seems bleak and foreboding, and you may not be able to imagine ever feeling well, normal, or happy again. You feel unlovable, and even if you know that people love you, you don't feel deserving of their love, your rationale being that if they knew the real you, they would stop loving you. Life becomes bitter and pointless, and you think a lot about death and dying. You may become so depressed that you imagine that death will release you from your hopelessness and despair. You may fantasize about not being alive or even about ending your life. You may even attempt to harm yourself and end your life.

Anxiety is somewhat different from depression but can be just as unbearable. It is the state where you feel overly and unduly worried, nervous or afraid, either for no realistic reason or to a degree that is out of proportion to the reality of the situation. Anxiety has physical symptoms where your heart speeds up and beats very fast, and it may feel as though it's going to beat right out of your chest. Your breathing quickens and becomes shallow and you may have the feeling that you are struggling for breath. Your throat may feel like its closing up and this is frightening. You can have stomachaches and headaches. You may feel dizzy and lightheaded and your ears may ring, your vision go blurry. You may sweat, shake and tremble, have pins and needles, and you may have to go to the bathroom often. You may feel disconnected from things around you and even from your own body.

You worry excessively and your imagination can run riot with all sorts of scary thoughts and fantasies. Worrying can keep you up at night, and nervous anticipation may paralyze you from activities you intend to carry out. All in all anxiety is very unpleasant and can make you feel even worse about yourself.

There is often some event, obvious or subtle, that brings on an episode of depression. You may lose someone of value to you. Your role in life may change: you may no longer be needed as a parent, employee, or partner. You may be rejected or experience the anguish of unrequited love. You may lose things that symbolize your value and worth like money, possessions, or prestige and status. In the face of these losses, setbacks and disappointments, you fall back on your deeply ingrained sense of low self-worth since these losses represent the disappearance of the external supplies of your positive self-worth.

At times like these—because of how you feel, because of the symptoms of stress and distress—you recognize something is not working and that you need help. You then turn to your doctor or dealer or other agent of distraction to help you blunt yourself to your emotional distress and pain.

THE MANY SYMPTOMS OF ALICE

For Alice, growing up in her family was a terrible experience. She felt from an early age that her parents, who were very religious, were hypocrites. She felt they were more interested in her obeying them and the rules of the church than they were in her. In fact, she felt that they didn't really care about her at all. They seemed much more interested in their public image (her father was a ranking lay member of their church) than in her and her welfare.

Alice described becoming rebellious from an early age. She was initially passive in her attempts to command her parents' attention and feigning illness was an effective method. As she got older, she became defiant and began to resist their injunctions openly. She reached a point in her early teens when she deliberately did the opposite of whatever her parents expected of her. She developed an interest in the occult, made friends with people her parents disapproved of, started to use drugs and dropped out of school.

Alice became an expert at shaming her parents and making them worry about her. They reacted with silent reproaches and the occasional lecture, which Alice had long since learned to disregard. The less affirmation she received from them, the harder she tried to force a genuine expression of concern, but to no avail. She eventually left home and took up with a man who abused her physically and emotionally for years. When the relationship ended, she missed it because despite its shortcomings, it was her closest experience of interest, affirmation and love.

Alice drifted from job to job, was chronically short of money, moved from one living arrangement to the next, continued to use drugs, and slept with whoever was available. She had no idea of what she wanted to do with her life or how to make it better. She expected solutions to come from others and did not know how to make positive and healthy changes in her life.

Alice invented more and more physical symptoms to engage others to care for her, an old strategy that had worked when she was younger. She was plagued with many psychosomatic complaints, depression and a dysfunctional personality, all of which stemmed from her inability to establish and maintain stable, intimate relationships with both herself and with others.

She lacked energy and could no longer experience pleasure, she became indifferent to her appearance and hygiene, her sleep was disturbed, she had no interest in social contact, and she had a general sense of purposelessness that often took the form of suicidal fantasies. She complained of lots of physical symptoms for which no physical causes were usually found.

Alice grew tired of her self-destructive lifestyle and wanted a different future. Through therapy, she became interested in learning how to stop blaming her past and instead started to learn how to take care of herself and take charge of her life.

Alice's many symptoms were characteristic of the symptoms of chronic depression that co-existed with her substance abuse and personality disorder. They can also be understood as symptomatic of being stuck in her failed low self-esteem and the despair and distress that arises from that state.

IS PERSONALITY NATURE OR NURTURE?

We have already established that poor parenting is not responsible for low self-esteem, and that regardless of whether you grow up in a loving or in an abusive home, you reach the same conclusion about your intrinsic lack of self-worth based on your narcissistic understanding of the times that your needs are not met which makes you feel overwhelmed. It is the coinciding of these two naturally occurring things that take place in every home and in every child's experience that leads to low self esteem.

This begs a question: does it matter whether children are treated like gold or abused? If you end up with low self-esteem regardless of the quality of your parenting, what does it matter whether you are treated lovingly or not? Why should it matter that you are neglected and abused if you develop low self-esteem anyhow? Why should your parents bother to parent you lovingly in the first place if it makes no difference to your self-esteem??

In fact, how you were treated and whether or not you were raised with love matters a great deal. It does not matter to the earliest conclusions you reach about your self-worth, but it matters crucially to how you go about solving the problem of your worthlessness. Whether or not you were loved and well treated is tremendously important to the specifics of how you learn to please, the degree to which you are likely to attain mastery over your preferred ways of pleasing, and the confidence you will develop in your ability to successfully please others. It has a huge influence on your ability to find ways to matter to yourself by mattering to others.

If you were raised in a loving and supportive home where your parents were responsive to you and your needs, and you were encouraged to please by developing behaviors and attitudes that are constructive and adaptive, then you will likely grow up confident and secure in the knowledge of your ability to please others and have them affirm you. You are more likely to be and to function as a confident, capable and productive person who fits in, gets along with others and builds stable relationships and a stable life. You are more likely to acquire the skills, values and behaviors that will equip you to become a supportive and constructive parent who will set your own children on a path of successful citizenship and parenthood.

By contrast, if your parents were hypercritical and undermining, indifferent or neglectful, you are less likely to emerge from childhood with these constructive and adaptive qualities. You will learn that your efforts to please are not very effective or reliable, and so you are more likely to be less secure or even insecure about your ability to induce others to value you.

Depending on the severity of the negative emotional environment at home and the degree to which you are unable to please your mother and have her validate you, you may emerge with an understanding that there is little you can do to make others value you, and have little to buffer your innate sense of worthlessness and so be at risk to develop symptoms and problems of failed low self esteem from an early age. You may tend to alienate rather than build intimacy in your relationships, be unstable in your moods, habits, and lifestyle, and become self-destructive as you focus on short-term fixes to soothe your toxic negative feelings. You will tend to be less realistic about the world as you personalize all of your disappointments and be more likely to make less satisfactory adjustments to it.

In psychiatry we refer to personality disorders and dysfunctional personality traits. These are the surface manifestations of your underlying inability to make your mother, and then the world, relate to you as though you mattered. The question is whether this inability to induce the world to value you is a function of your early environment or your innate capacity to learn and influence your surroundings.

One way of addressing this question is by referring to the classic debate of nature versus nurture—in other words, whether your innate capacities (nature) are more or less important than the environment in which you are raised (nurture) for being responsible for your personality. The approach that appeals to me is to view personality development as a function of the ways in which the forces of nature and of nurture combine to shape the person you become. With respect to the self-esteem aspects of personality, specific natural factors include the natural experience of Humpty Dumpty style abandonment and the narcissistic stage of cognitive development. These combine with the specific and individual conditions of your unique circumstances, which represent the nurture or environmental influences on self-esteem. Your personality comes together in response to the interaction and combination of these factors. It would make sense biologically for personality to be flexible and to arise from collaboration between the forces of nature and nurture, as this would give the organism a better chance of adapting to and surviving in the environment, especially in a changing environment.

While these deliberations make for interesting discussions, the important thing to remember is that symptoms are symptoms and not the problem itself. When you have symptoms, they are drawing attention to an underlying problem. Your task, and the task of the professionals from whom you seek help, is to get to the bottom of the problems that produce the symptoms in the first place. It should not be enough to merely get rid of the symptoms without fixing the underlying problem that brought them to your attention.

In A Nutshell

- Failing low self-esteem is stressful and leads to many different symptoms of distress

- These result in various diagnostic labels such as Mood Disorders, Major Depressive Disorder, Anxiety Disorders and Personality Disorders

- Recognize that symptoms are just symptoms and not the problem itself; they point to an underlying problem that you need to identify and fix if you can

---

CHAPTER 10

THE HIGH VALUE OF LOW SELF-ESTEEM

"Why do you have to be a nonconformist like everybody else?"

— James Thurber

In earlier chapters I talked about the way you come to know yourself as a separate self. You will recall that the first thing you come to know about yourself as a separate being is that you are less than and inferior to others. Shortly after you come to the conclusion that you are worthless, unlovable and not worth your mother's while to care for you and keep you alive. You realize that if you don't do anything to make her care for you, your needs will not be met and you'll be overwhelmed and die.

This is not an auspicious start to a life of healthy self-esteem. In response to this you learn ways to make others care for and value you, and to the degree to which they do, you are able to feel worthwhile, to enjoy positive self-esteem.

When you find that the ways you have learned to make others value you stop working, and you cannot get back on track, you face your inner worthlessness head on. This is unbearable: it leads to misery, depression and even suicide. You may start to drink or use drugs and may end up on antidepressants.

I have also proposed that in modern times, it is increasingly likely that more and more people will reach a point when their ability to keep making the world value them fails. The external sources and supplies for their positive self-regard dry up, and they revert to their original disposition of worthlessness. So more and more people are finding their way to Prozac and other chemicals. This begs a few questions: Why are we set up to fail? Why don't we see ourselves as intrinsically worthwhile instead of intrinsically worthless? Why aren't we naturally happy and content instead of anxious and depressed? Would the world be a worse place if we had positive self-worth? What purpose is served by being universally primed for Prozac? How is it that normal childhood development leads us to a state where we are at constant risk of depression rather than in a positive, dependable and life affirming state?

Imagine an experiment involving a generation of children in some distant time in the past. At age three half the members are programmed to pose the questions "Why is my mother not here when I need her? Why am I overwhelmed and falling apart? Why is my existence threatened? What can I do to protect myself?" The other half are programmed to ask the questions when they are older and old enough to have acquired the cognitive ability to decenter or think objectively.

The two groups' responses to the questions would be very different. The three-year-olds are still in their narcissistic stage of cognitive development—where they cannot yet decenter—and the only way they can answer these questions is narcissistically, in terms of themselves, from their own immediate and direct experience, and not in terms of a perspective different from their own. So when their mother is absent, they understand her absence to be about them rather than about her and they conclude, wrongly, that they are not worth their mother's while, that they are worthless and unlovable. This is how the primal condition of low self-esteem emerges.

The older children who can decenter understand their mothers' absence differently. They understand the real reasons for their mothers' absence and that her absence is not because of them or their lack of worth. They have no reason to conclude that they are worthless and so conclude instead that they are worthy and worth caring about — and acquire the state of inherently high self-esteem.

The difference then between those who develop high rather than low self-esteem comes down to when they pose the question of their mother's absence. Those who ask the question before they are able to decenter—the cognitive narcissists—develop low self-esteem, while those who pose the question once they can decenter – the cognitive realists - develop high self-esteem.

If equal numbers of these children are programmed to ask this question before and after acquiring the ability to decenter, then equal numbers of intrinsically high self-esteemers and low self-esteemers make up the population.

How will these low and high self-esteemers fare over time? Remember that low self-esteemers come up with a solution to the problem of not being cared for by learning to please their mothers. The things that please their mothers are generally the behaviors, skills, attitudes and values that are pleasing to other members of the community as well as to their mothers. So in learning to please their mothers they end up learning how to please and therefore how to fit in with their community, because what pleases their mother is usually pleasing to other adults. Most mothers are pleased when they observe their children fitting in and doing what is expected of them and it is unusual for a mother to be displeased by her child behaving in ways that conform to the social norms of the group. In learning to please their mothers and also others, the low self-esteemers are learning the conventions, rules and norms of social interaction that promote social cohesion. In this way low self-esteem promotes social learning.

Social learning is adaptive because the more easily group members learn to fit in and co-operate with each other, the less group resources have to be devoted to ensuring compliance to group norms and so the more resources are available for other important survival activities and functions. Low self-esteem creates an internal motivation for social learning that frees the group to concentrate on other survival activities. Low self-esteem is therefore an ingenious psychological device with biological benefits for both individual and group survival.

High self-esteemers do not have this same inner need to please or motivation to learn as low self-esteemers, and so are less likely to learn the social codes and conventions of healthy and adaptive social interaction, and less likely to fit in. The group will have to devote more resources to ensure their co-operation, and so fewer resources will be available for other survival activities. Groups dominated with innate high self-esteemers will be at a disadvantage because they will be investing more in getting members to co-operate and less on the actual tasks required for survival.

It is an interesting paradox that the cognitive narcissism that drives you to please others, makes you more sensitive to the needs of others and so, in a sense, less narcissistic or self-centered in your behavior. By contrast, those who are cognitively realistic are more inclined to behave selfishly towards others because they do not need to please them and are less likely to worry about what others think of them.

Low self-esteem, then, encourages and drives social learning, conformity, and cohesive social functioning, whereas high self-esteem leans in the opposite direction - toward social disruption, chaos and more risky social survival.

So considering these two hypothetical groups, the low and high self-esteemers, let's look at which group gains the upper hand, genetically speaking, and how it does so.

Imagine that you are a woman in this hypothetical community and that you are being courted by prospective suitors. Imagine too that you have a free hand to choose your mate, and your choice comes down to two individuals who are identical in all respects except that one has innate high self-esteem and the other has innate low self-esteem.

Most people in this situation would choose the high self-esteemer because high self-esteem sounds far more attractive than low self-esteem. But remember that a high self-esteemer has no need to please and is therefore less likely to act in ways that are pleasing. Since the high self-esteemer is less likely to care what you think of him and less likely to try to please you, he is more likely to literally love and leave you, and again, literally leave you holding the baby.

On the other hand, the low self-esteemer needs to please you, has a strong inner psychological drive to please you, and so is more likely to act in ways that are pleasing to you. The low self-esteemer is less likely to love and leave you, and more likely to stick around help you raise the baby rather than leave you holding it and fending for you and the baby on your own.

In the sense that low self-esteemers try to please, they likely make better lovers and better suitors than innate high self-esteemers. They are more inclined to be considerate and less likely to be selfish.

Considering the enormous investment and risks a woman undertakes in gestating and birthing a child, as a mother, you would be interested in choices that increased the chances that your children would survive and grow to adulthood. Low self-esteemers offer you a much better chance of accomplishing this, whereas high self-esteemers are more likely to leave you in the lurch and thereby reduce your chances of successfully raising your young. You do better by choosing a low self-esteem mate, even if he is superficially less appealing than his high self-esteem counterparts.

Making babies is just the first part of the gene's quest to get where it wants to go, which is to the next generation. Equally important in getting the gene to its destination is rearing, or raising the offspring to adulthood so they can reproduce and produce the next generation. Rearing in this sense requires that the parents keep the child safe, provides sufficient food and nourishment, and teaches the child what they will need to know in order to reproduce and successfully rear their own children.

The low self-esteemer needs to please, and so is likely to try to please the other adults that he or she depends on, and so is more likely to listen to, obey and try to emulate these elders. They are therefore more likely to learn from their elders. What they learn will be how to do things, how to do the tasks upon which their survival depends. They will be more likely to learn the necessities of hunting, gathering, farming, animal husbandry and so on as low self-esteemers because of their need to please. If you think of these dynamics as being developed and refined thousands of years ago—before the age of supermarkets, agribusiness, and the overproduction we are now capable of in our modern world—you will appreciate that in the hunter-gatherer and early pastoral times, survival was by no means a sure thing. Learning from the experience of your elders was the best way to equip yourself with the knowledge and tools for survival. The reverence that earlier societies had for their elders attests to this dependence on them.

High self-esteemers have no or less need to please, are less likely to try to please, and so are less likely to listen, obey and emulate their elders. They are therefore less likely to learn the things they need to know to be able to rear their young, so fewer of their offspring will survive to the point where they can in turn, reproduce and rear their own young.

Low self-esteemers make better students than high self-esteemers, and so are better equipped to provide for their young and raise them to adulthood. Low self-esteemers make better lovers, which makes them more successful suitors and parents. This is all because of their internal and psychological need to please, which high self-esteemers do not have.

The advantages of low self-esteem would have been more persuasive earlier on in human history when survival was less reliable and more tenuous. While these advantages seem less impressive to us in modern times, because survival is more assured, even small advantages earlier on would have translated into major benefits in times of greater threat and when survival was less assured. Given the advantages low self-esteemers have over high self-esteemers, it stands to reason that after a few generations low self-esteem and the (psychological) mechanisms that promote it would have been selected. More low self-esteemers would have entered the gene pool, and eventually low self-esteemers would have dominated to the point that low self-esteem became the norm and high self-esteem the exception.

Low self-esteem is, at least for social creatures, a biological necessity, an invaluable means of ensuring survival and the passage of genes from one generation to the next. In contrast, high self-esteem brings significant disadvantages for genetic survival because of the way high self-esteemers lean away from social learning and conformity, thereby reducing their chances of successful courtship and procreation, rearing and therefore survival.

To conclude this imaginary exercise of a young woman free to choose her suitor, perhaps after a some trial and error she is most likely to come to the conclusion that her genes and those of her off spring are best served by a low self-esteemer than by his high self-esteem counterpart.

THE SOCIAL ADVANTAGES OF LOW SELF-ESTEEM

The adaptive disadvantages of high self-esteem can be detrimental to the survival of social groups. One can consider that small social groups have historically had a more precarious hold on survival than larger groups. In the sense that small, more homogeneous groups command fewer resources and fewer adaptive coping and survival strategies than larger and more heterogeneous groups, they can be considered more vulnerable to the vagaries of nature. So the survival of smaller groups depends more on their capacity to focus most of their energies and resources on the tasks of production and survival, rather than enforcing conformity and cooperation among its members.

The disruption that high self-esteemers introduce into the group, by virtue of their lower emotional investment in conforming to the group's norms and requirements, distracts the group from its productive tasks, thus placing its survival in jeopardy. When the group has to expend its energies and resources keeping the high self-esteemers in check, its capacity to function smoothly and effectively is likely to be compromised. This may have dire consequences for the group, such as unrest, civil war, or even extinction.

The adaptive disadvantages of high self-esteem are perhaps more hidden in our modern societies, where group survival is less tenuous. Our societies have evolved to the point where we are able to store food and produce more than we need, so we are not as dependent on meeting basic needs. The threat to group survival posed by innate high self-esteemers is not as apparent as with smaller groups, whose existence is more marginal. High self-esteemers, in the sense of their being nonconformist and potentially beyond the law—or criminal—in our time poses more of a threat to individuals than to the group as a whole, because of the group's far greater "carrying capacity" for nonconformists and outlaws.

It is perhaps more difficult to appreciate the high value of low self-esteem in this day and age because its advantages are hidden, thanks to the negative connotations of conformity and our reverence for antiheroes and rebels. From a biological perspective, however, conformity, cooperation, and respect for elders (which corresponds to learning from them) have always been and remain crucial to successful adaptation and survival. The institution of laws that govern social relations, together with our continuing cultural respect for the law as a central source of social order and stability, highlights this crucial relationship between survival and social cohesion.

So the point about low self-esteem is that through the mechanism of needing to please, it drives social learning and eases social function, enhancing the chances of social survival. The manner whereby low self-esteem comes into being is highly efficient. It's internally derived from developmental processes, requires no effort or resources from the group, and frees up group energies and resources for survival tasks. Low self-esteem is, then, a highly adaptive characteristic for social existence and survival.

MIDLIFE CRISIS

In contemporary society, once you have raised your children and they leave home to start their own families, once you reach your peak as a provider and realize you are unlikely to be able to provide more or advance further in your career, or once you retire or become unemployable, you lose your ability to make the world affirm you through your efforts, and you confront once again your inner worthlessness. This causes you to feel bad and you feel gloomy and sad, worried, frightened, miserable and depressed. The situation is sometimes referred to as a midlife crisis.

Does it matter that you become miserable and depressed? Well, it certainly matters to you, because those feelings are painful. You don't like them and you want them to stop. But from an evolutionary point of view, once you have fulfilled your duty by transmitting your genes to the next generation and successfully rearing your offspring to the point where they can reproduce the generation after them, it does not matter if you are depressed; your feelings are no longer relevant to the forces of evolution. From that point on, you are expendable.

Some cultures make room for their members who have passed the stage of reproduction as mentors to the younger and newer generations. In these roles, individuals who have gone beyond their reproductive stage remain valued members of their group by playing valuable roles as conveyors of the culture, teachers and transmitters of the knowledge and wisdoms required for social survival.

In contemporary society, with all the changes to our social structures, these roles are no longer as readily available, and the opportunity for mid- and late-lifers to take on new constructive social roles has diminished. Midlife as well as late-life crisis is an ever-increasing problem that coincides with rising rates of depression and suicide with advancing age.

Richard's story illustrates this loss of esteem through the loss of a productive role. Having sold his business and happily entered retirement, Richard found that the pleasure he anticipated from doing all the things he planned did not materialize. He felt increasingly flat and empty. He missed his old job and his colleagues. Instead of getting out on his boat, golfing, or hanging out at the coffee bars with friends, he found himself moping around at home.

Without his long-established and familiar routines for earning regard from others through his work, he slipped into a depression (much to the consternation of his wife, who was still working). Richard's jovial and upbeat nature was replaced with a morose, brooding, and anxious persona; he was a stranger to both himself and his wife. He sought treatment for this depression and was prescribed antidepressants. They didn't help; instead they made him feel worse, because of the fifteen pounds weight gain they caused.

Richard became interested in understanding himself psychologically as a way of feeling better. During therapy he gained an understanding of how his dependence on others for positive self-worth originated and how it had served him throughout his working life. He also came to understand how these external sources of self-worth came to a halt with his retirement, and how he could learn to become his own source of worth and to value himself for his own sake instead of for his accomplishments. He found this change refreshing and liberating, and his depression disappeared.

Erica, on the other hand, went to extremes to hang onto her role as a mother, her almost exclusive means of earning positive self-regard and esteem. It was a vain and self-destructive pursuit. Erica was a single mom who had always had a difficult relationship with her son, her only child. He was always hard to please and difficult to console. As he got older he became critical and demanding of her and she could do no right by him. He moved away after school and rarely contacted her. He became a drug addict and demanded cash from her in a manner that was cruel and demeaning. Erica, who longed for a wholesome relationship with him, gave in to his demands. But as her finances were limited, she could not always give him money, and he maintained a distant and manipulative connection with her that hurt her deeply. Erica was increasingly distraught and eventually became depressed and suicidal, and came to the clinic for treatment.

She believed that she had failed as a mother, and felt that her life was over. Her son was the most important thing in her life and she felt she had nothing else to live for. Unfortunately, her sole interest was learning how to make him relate to her in a more gratifying way. She was not interested to learn about herself or about how to deal realistically with her son. As a result, she dropped out of treatment, as miserable and desperate as she was before.

She was stuck in failed low self-esteem, brought on by the loss of her major means of earning self worth, which was by nurturing her child who had grown up and no longer needed her maternal care.

In A Nutshell

- Low self-esteem provokes a need to please others

- Behaviours that are pleasing to others make for co-operative social interactions and relationships

- Low self-esteem thus promotes social learning, social cohesion and ultimately survival and is therefore a highly adaptive trait in humans

PART TWO:

PUTTINGWHATYOU'VE LEARNED INTO PRACTICE

CHAPTER 11

TRANSCENDING LOW SELF-ESTEEM

"I know who I was when I got up this morning, but I think I must have been changed several times since then."

— *Lewis Carroll, Alice in Wonderland*

What can be done about this state of failing low self-esteem when it stops serving your interests and instead begins to undermine you and your well being? How can you mitigate your low self-esteem once it has served its purpose of spurring you to learn to fit in with your family and your social surroundings? What can you do once your low self-esteem becomes a burden rather than a constructive force? How do you deal with the problems that arise from failing low self-esteem—problems like depression and anxiety, failing intimate relationships, patterns of disappointment, hurt, and conflict in your relationships, workaholism and burnout, alcoholism or drug, food, or other addictions? How do you reverse the cycle of fruitless attempts to boost your ego that only end up causing you more grief? Is it possible to get beyond the pitfalls of negative self-esteem and achieve positive self-esteem and a healthy sense of self-worth?

The following two vignettes illustrate what people can achieve once they are prepared to give up their pursuit of external sources of validation and find new ways to overcome their failing low self-esteem.

GRAHAM GIVES UP ON GLAMOUR

Graham was in his early thirties, single, and financially well off. He was a self-starter who dropped out of university as soon as his father died. His university education had always been his father's idea, and Graham had attended only to stay in his father's good graces. Graham's father was aloof and emotionally distant, though his mother was emotionally present and supportive. Graham blamed his father for the emotional difficulties and frustrating behavior patterns he experienced as an adult.

Graham was dashingly handsome and could be very charming, especially toward women. He was physically fit and active, spending much of his free time doing extreme sports. Through his activities, he met a steady stream of attractive and sporty romantic partners and was serially monogamous.

But Graham felt unable to have satisfactory relationships with women. He always chose beautiful but emotionally and financially needy lovers who became dependent on him. He would generously provide for them, and in return expected their gratitude and an on-demand supply of affirmation. Things always started off well; Graham would be charming, attentive and supportive, and would dazzle his girlfriends with his generosity. He was highly attuned to their needs and provided reliably for them, but when his lovers did not meet his needs, and when he did not receive their approval in exchange for what he gave them, he became frustrated and upset and flew into rages. This behavior would poison the relationships and bring them to an end. This recurring pattern made him so despondent and desperate that he sought psychiatric help.

When Graham arrived at the mood disorders clinic, he was lonely, bitter, and depressed. He felt that time was passing him by, and that he ought to be more settled, specifically in a stable and gratifying marriage. The fact that he was still single was deeply distressing to him. He often found it hard to motivate himself to get things done. He could not tolerate being on his own and felt despondent in his own company and felt bad about his destructive rages. Even though he appreciated the rich and full life he led, he knew that his emotions and behaviors were not normal or healthy, and he frequently felt that life was not worth living.

Graham came to recognize that his low self-esteem played a central role in his patterns of investing heavily in pleasing his partners and expecting their affection and affirmation in return. He came to understand that it was not the dynamics of his family, specifically his father, that caused his low self-esteem, but rather how his experience of his family had reinforced his preexisting sense of worthlessness.

He learned that his father's aloofness was not a reflection of his lack of worth, but was simply the way his father was. His father, for his own reasons, was not a warm or emotionally fuzzy kind of guy, but was instead a reserved and anxious man who worried about his children getting ahead in life. Graham came to understand how he had personalized his father's strictness and lack of warmth, how he had misinterpreted it to mean that he, Graham, was not worth being loved, that he was unlovable. He understood that he had thought of himself as unlovable for as long as he could remember. He came to understand how his cognitive narcissism led him to misinterpret impersonal events (his father's coldness, his girlfriends' lack of reciprocity) as if they were personal—as if they were all about him—and how distorting that had been for his identity and reinforced his sense of low self-worth.

Graham gained insight into how he had taught himself to cope with this sense of being unlovable by making himself desirable. He worked hard at being seen as a caring, loving person, so that he would be loved and cared for in return. He made himself indispensable to others with his attentiveness and kindness, on the unspoken understanding that recipients of his generosity would treat him as a beloved and treasured person. He came to understand the source of his frustration and rage he felt when his thoughtfulness was not reciprocated, which helped him understand its unreasonableness. He came to realize that others were not responsible for his feelings of worth and that he did not have to manipulate others to think of him as worthwhile. He came to appreciate that depending on others for a sense of worth was unpredictable and disempowering and that he was responsible for his own self-worth and no one else's, just as no one else was responsible for his.

Graham also came to appreciate the dynamics of how he chose beautiful, emotionally needy women to make him look and feel good, and that when they let him down by not meeting his expectations and needs, he responded like a frustrated and impotent child. He reached an understanding that his rage and misery, his expectations and reactions, and how he felt about himself, his sense of self worth, were all his responsibility and that it he, and only he, not anyone else, was responsible for him.

As he learned all this and grew emotionally, Graham found himself making different choices about the women he dated. He began passing on beautiful, dramatic, and emotionally chaotic women with lots of problems for him to fix, the women he had been drawn to before. He found himself far more attracted to calm, self-sufficient women who were not waiting for Prince Charming to ride up and rescue them. While he still didn't particularly care for his own company, he no longer interpreted it as evidence of his inherent lack of worth and unlovability. He reached a point where he took on the responsibility of being himself, and began to put that into practice. He began to more fully appreciate the richness of his life, of being alive and found that there was no longer anything to be enraged by, and that nothing made life not worth living.

SONIA AND THE ART OF THE POLITE NO

Sonia was a young woman with a long past. She was raised by an abusive alcoholic father and a passive, ineffectual mother who was unable to protect her from her father's verbal abuse and physical beatings. From an early age, Sonia's father told her repeatedly that she was useless and would not amount to anything. In her teens, she was sexually molested by her father's drunken friends. Her self-image was shocking: she believed that she was worthless and that she deserved all the mistreatment she received.

Sonia was so desperate for attention and approval that she became promiscuous and slept with anyone who showed the slightest interest in her. She fooled herself into believing that these minor displays of interest were signs of love and lovability, even though she knew it wasn't true. Her fears of being alone, which to her meant being worthless, were so fierce that she went to great lengths to attract attention, dressing and behaving provocatively, seducing strangers, and never saying no to anything asked of her.

She received drugs and sex but no love or intimacy from this lifestyle. She got locked into a vicious cycle of feeling worthless, behaving self-destructively, feeling even more worthless and behaving even more self-destructively. The unhappier she was, the more she sought comfort in drugs and the arms of strangers. Her judgment of suitable lovers was so appalling that on more than one occasion she found herself literally looking down the barrel of a gun the morning after.

Sonia's inability to say no compromised her in other situations, not only ones involving sex and drugs. Her need to please was so great that she was unable to set boundaries around the demands friends and especially ex-boyfriends made of her time and resources. Her generosity was repeatedly exploited; she was a pushover to all who knew her.

Sonia was diagnosed with depression, was treated with antidepressants and saw different counselors—but to no avail. During treatment at the mood disorder clinic, with the focus on her self-esteem, Sonia learned that blaming her father was keeping her trapped in a negative view of herself. She came to see how her self-destructive search for affirmation was doomed to failure. She came to appreciate that it was up to her to define her worth, regardless of how others treated or thought of her, and regardless of her past, what had happened to her and what she had and hadn't done. She came to appreciate that the way others treated her had to do with them and who they were and were not about her and her worth or lack of worth. She realized that just because others treated her disrespectfully did not mean that she was not worthy of respect; it just meant that she tolerated being treated badly by others and that she could stop and change that.

Sonia saw that she had choices around how to define herself and her self-worth, and she recognized the advantages of taking control of her self-image. She came to understand that she was not responsible for the behavior of others in the past, but was responsible for her own feelings, thoughts, and behaviors. She could decide what to think and what to do with her feelings. She could decide how to behave, and what she did and didn't want to do. She realized she could change her mind, and that because she had chosen one course of action the day before, she didn't have to choose it today or tomorrow. She was responsible for her decisions and choices and her changes of heart and of mind. It was up to her to determine how she felt about herself and her life, not up to anybody else—not her father, his friends, nor the dreadful men she picked up in bars. She came to see that there was a more realistic basis by which to determine her self-worth, different from the distorted ways she read her worth off the ways that others treated her.

Sonia started to make different choices about who she let into her bed and into her life. She practiced saying no and found that she felt good about herself when she exercised good judgment. She refined the art of the polite no. And by giving up on destructive relationships with unstable men, she stopped undermining herself. She put a halt to friends taking advantage of her generosity, which was always a disguise for her desperation. Her moods improved, and she was no longer in a state of constant panic at the prospect of abandonment. She made peace with herself and discovered that she had nothing to fear.

CHAPTER 12

INFORMED DECISION MAKING

"You've got to do your own growing, no matter how tall your grandfather was."

— *Irish proverb*

Both Graham and Sonia, in their own ways and for their own reasons, were determined to escape from the trap of failed low self-esteem and found a way to do it. The question is, how did they manage it?

Understanding that failed low self-esteem is at the root of much of your distress prepares you to target that failed low self-esteem and combat its unhappy effects. To put an end to depression, anxiety, panic, and despair, you need to learn how to retool your self-image and sense of self-worth. In building a new and improved self-image, you put a stop to your self-defeating patterns of overwork, failed relationships, conflicts, drug and alcohol abuse, reliance on medications, dependence on others to fix you, and other self-defeating and self-destructive behavior patterns.

The way to change, to get beyond failed and failing low self-esteem, is by making an informed decision to be different.

There are two parts to the idea of making an informed decision. The first is the informed part, which refers to information you need in order to make a decision. Since knowledge is power, the chances are that a decision that is not based on information will likely not be powerful or lasting whereas one based on information specific to the issue at hand will be powered to become meaningful and to last.

Without the relevant information, a decision to change is toothless; and without the decision, there is no mechanism for change. What follows next is the information required for change and what is involved in the decision to change. What is up for change is the reliance on others for your self worth, to be replaced by yourself as the source of your worth.

YOU HAVE THE POWER

There are two distinct things you need to know to become your own source of worth. The first is an understanding of how your reliance on others for your worth came about in the first place. And the second is an understanding of the real nature of reality and the world as opposed to the narcissistically distorted view of the world that dates back to your early days when your thinking and understanding was egocentric.

The understanding of how your self-worth evolved and how you came to depend on others for positive self-esteem is what has been discussed in earlier sections of the book. Understanding this evolutionary pathway of self-esteem means that you can appreci-ate three specific aspects that are necessary to making a decision to change.

In understanding your self-esteem you firstly appreciate that it was you who decided that you were worthless. In the privacy of your own mind and in a way that you were unable to express or give voice to, you decided at the age of three that that you were worthless. No one told you that you were. Had anyone told you that you were worthless before then, you would not have understood them, and by the time you could have, you had already decided that you were worthless. Regardless of what did or didn't happen to you in your early childhood, you reached this conclusion because of your expe-rience of being overwhelmed by your needs that were sometimes not met in a timely way, and your narcissistic way of understanding this experience of being overwhelmed. These two universal experi-ences led you to conclude that you were worthless. You reached this conclusion on your own, you made up this belief, and you were the author of your beliefs about your lack of worth. No one did it to or for you.

Since you are the author of your beliefs, you then have the 'autho-rial voice' to change the beliefs if you choose. It is up to you and only you to rewrite the script. If no one else authored them for you—if no one else made you worthless—then it's not up to anyone else to make you worthwhile. You have the power to make yourself the way you want to be. It is within your power to change your view of your-self and your self-worth, just as it was within your power to create these beliefs about yourself when you were three.

It is not up to anyone else to make you different or to change your view of your self and your worth since no—one else made you think the way you do or be the way you are. Others are responsible for their beliefs and for themselves, not for you. Which is just as well because if it were up to others to change you and to make you worthwhile, and they didn't or couldn't, you'd be stuck and powerless to change. So it is fortunate that change is not in anyone's hands but your own, and being the person with the greatest interest in yourself and being the way you'd like to be, it's just as well that it is you that has the power to change yourself and not anyone else.

The second thing you appreciate once you understand how your self-esteem came about is that when you authored your beliefs about your inherent lack of worth, you did so in ignorance. You were young and dumb. You were three years old. Your thinking and understanding were narcissistic. You had no other way to make sense of your experience other than by personalizing it. You were unable to know the real reasons for your mother's absences, and inaccurately attributed them to you and to your inherent lack of worth. Your narcissistic worldview was grossly inaccurate and flawed. It's true that your mother was not always there when you needed her, but it was not because you were not worth her while; it was for reasons that had nothing to do with you and your worth. Her absences were due to the realities of normal healthy separation but you couldn't understand that then. The conclusions you reached about your lack of worth were based on misinformation and poor quality and narcissistically distorted data, and so were inaccurate and simply wrong.

Once you are armed with more accurate and more reliable information, you are free to reach different conclusions based on this more accurate information. You can now understand things realistically and can appreciate that your mother's absences were about her and the realities of her day, and not because of your lack of worth. You are free to reach a different conclusion about your worth knowing what you now know about her absences. You are free, if you choose, to be worthwhile rather than worthless. As authors of your beliefs, you are free to use better quality information to reach a different conclusion about your worth.

150

So, you're the author of your beliefs and are now equipped with better quality information to make a decision about your worth. What else do you need to know?

In understanding the origins of your self-esteem you can appreciate that even though you reached this conclusion in ignorance, you did so out of necessity. You did not decide you were worthless because there was anything wrong with you, or because you were somehow flawed or defective; on the contrary, you reached this conclusion as a matter of biological and genetic necessity. Deciding that you were worthless led you to try to please others in order to have your needs met, and this was an extremely efficient and effective way of getting you to learn the things you need to know in order to fit in and survive in your community. Instead of worthlessness being a blemish or flaw, it is an ingenious and brilliant way for social creatures to accomplish their genetic goal to get their genes to the next generation.

It may appear contradictory to state, on the one hand, that you made the decision to be worthless, and on the other, to say that you had no choice, that it was developmentally and biologically determined. It seems to me that both views are accurate. The circumstances under which you made this decision were not within your control; you could and did not control your mother's absences, nor did you control your thinking capacities. Nor did you have any control over the adaptive advantages that arose for you and your social network as a result of your decision. In spite of this lack of control, it was you and you alone who formed the notion of your worthlessness, because no one forced, pressured, or persuaded you to reach that conclusion; it was you and you alone who drew this conclusion from your experiences and from your ability to make sense of them.

So knowing how your conviction about your worthlessness came about, you can appreciate that it was you who invented the belief in the first place, that you did so in ignorance and based on faulty information, and that you did so out of a biological necessity rather than because there was anything wrong with you. Knowing this puts you in a position to make a different decision about your worth, especially once you have better quality and more accurate and reliable information.

But there is something else you need to know before you are ready to make a different decision about your worth.

NONNARCISSISTIC REALITY

Your conclusion about being worthless was based on your narcissistic misunderstanding of reality: you are the center of the world; the world is all about you; whatever happens to you is about you; the world exists for you; it either gratifies or frustrates you in terms of whether you like or don't like your experiences. Through the narcissistic lens you personalize everything that you experience as though it were all about you.

Chicken Little, the chicken who ran around crying that the sky was falling when an acorn fell on his head, exemplifies this narcissistic worldview. Chicken Little, a child, has no capacity to appreciate anything beyond his immediate experience, so when an acorn falls on his head, and he sees the sky above his head, it means to him that the sky is falling. Since he does not see the acorn, it does not exist. He sees the sky so the sky is falling.

Non-narcissistic, or actual, reality is different. In real reality, things happen in the world that have nothing to do with you, even if they affect you. The reason things happen to and around you is not because of you and your worth or lack of worth; they happen because they just happen for all the different reasons that things happen in the world. The world is not a personal world even though you experience it personally.

The simple truth about the world is that it is impersonal and indifferent. The world does not exist for you and is not here because of or for you. You happen to be alive in the world. That's all. You come and go, but the world endures. You will eventually die and be forgotten, but the world will continue to exist. The few people who know and care about you will also die and be forgotten. You will mean as little to your great grandchildren as your great grandparents mean to you. You are just passing through.

And whether in your passage you are happy or sad, rich or poor, kind or nasty, upstanding or criminal, fat or thin, quick or slow, distinguished or undistinguished, you will die just the same and be forgotten just the same. The truth is that you are of no consequence to the world. It existed and functioned before you arrived and will continue to do so long after you depart.

The world is as it is, not as it is for me. The world appears flat to me, but is round, despite how it seems to me, despite how I experience it.

This is the realistic and impersonal view of the world, the exact opposite of the narcissistic view of the world, in which you see yourself as the center of the universe, and things happen 'for a reason', meaning a reason personal to you, because the universe is trying to teach you a lesson, as if the universe cared whether you were one way or another.

In making a decision about your worth, you will see why it is important to remember that the universe is impersonal and indifferent rather than narcissistically personal.

The other important aspect of reality to recognize is that the world is comprised of an infinite variety of things, of objects and forces, and that in our lives we are exposed to some of them. Some of what happens in the world impinges on us. Most of what happens doesn't. Things exist across spectrums, from light to dark, hot to cold, big to small, short to tall, near to far, sweet to sour, pleasant to painful. The universe is made up of an infinite variety of different things or phenomena that exist across these spectrums.

And humans are discerning beings and prefer some conditions to others, as do all life forms. Humans have likes and dislikes; it is our nature to have preferences. You may prefer sunny to overcast, hot to cold, dry to wet, blue to pink, Coke to Pepsi, chocolate to rhubarb, or person A to person B.

The point is that your preferences are merely your preferences. They are about what you like and are not cosmic judgments about the value of things. That you prefer one thing to another doesn't mean that the one is any more or less valuable in its essence just because of how you feel about it. And similarly, just because someone's else's feelings and preferences about you don't make you more or less valuable, according to their preference.

This is what we know about the real world for sure. You can absolutely count on as fact that during your life, some of your preferences will be met, and others won't be. You will get to experience some of the things you like. And some of the things you prefer to happen will not. This is guaranteed.

In addition, some of the things you'd prefer to not happen will not happen. And some of those things you'd like to not happen will. This is the case because the world is not here to either gratify or frustrate you, it is just highly varied and you will be exposed to the randomness of life. People cannot control what happens to them, although all people try to influence their experience. You direct your attention and effort so that you avoid the things you don't want and are more likely to encounter the things you do. You have more or less influence on what happens to you, depending on the circumstances, but you do not control it. All you do control is how you are with what happens to you, but not what happens.

Now you know what you need to know to make a decision about being worthwhile, that seeing beyond the limits of your narcissistic lens, the world is varied, indifferent, and impersonal, and that it is not here to either frustrate or gratify you, despite the fact that some of your preferences will be satisfied while others won't be.

THE DECISION

The decision to be worthwhile is an existential decision. In a sense, you already made this decision a long time ago. The question to be answered is whether life is worth living.

You already posed and answered this question for yourself. Likely long ago. You probably answered it like this: yes, life is worth living, but only on condition that it gives me what I want—or enough of what I want, and not what I don't want, or little enough of what I don't want. As long as life conforms to my preferences, it is worth having.

This is as you can appreciate, a deeply narcissistic view of the value of life, because it hinges on your particular experience of life and the degree to which you are fulfilled or disappointed. Life needs to suit your tastes in order to be worth having, as though life were here to satisfy and gratify you personally – this is cognitive narcissism at its finest.

This attitude about whether life is worth living is conditional: as long as life meets your conditions, it is worth having. If and when it does not meet your conditions, it becomes not worth having. As long as you get what you want, life's great; when you don't get what you want or get what you don't want or lose what you had, life becomes not worth living.

If the world treats you as though you matter, then the world, or life, is worth having. When you don't experience validation from the world, and you get what you don't want instead of what you do, life is not worth having and you contemplate giving up on life. If you're worthwhile, life is worth having. The opposite is true too, that suicidal thoughts about life not being worth living arise when your conditions are not met and you experience yourself as worthless.

This conditional view of life arises early in your cognitive development. When the conditions of your life suit you, you and your life are worthwhile and you have no reason to question your conditional acceptance of life. It is only when the conditions of your life do not suit you that the possibility of re-opening this question arises.

But if you step beyond the conditional narcissistic framework you can answer the question differently. You can choose to answer the question realistically rather than narcissistically. You can say to yourself: look here, the world is impersonal and indifferent, it is not about me even though I experience it, so I can choose to value life unconditionally rather than conditionally; I can choose to value life on life's terms rather than on my terms; I can choose to value living life for life's sake rather than for mine; and I can choose to value life as it is, rather than as it for me.

Because you are capable of decentering and of realistic thinking, you are free to answer the question in this way. Or not.

Obviously this is a question only you can ask of and answer for yourself. It is a question between you and you. It is your private conversation with yourself.

How does choosing to value life unconditionally on life's terms affect your self-esteem? Let's say that you make the decision to value life realistically, for life's sake, on life's terms. This means that you decide that life is worth having on life's terms, not on yours. Now, if you decide that life is worth having regardless of your experience, that means that your life is worth having regardless of the conditions. If your life is worth having, then obviously you are worth having your life. And if you are worth having your life, then you are worthwhile.

This is how you come to be worthwhile, and the source of your own worth. This is how you acquire healthy and positive self-esteem.

You make a new and different decision about your worth, a decision that is based on a realistic understanding of the nature of the world rather than the one you made so many years ago that was based on an ill-informed and narcissistically distorted view of reality. This decision is based on sound and accurate information about the nature of reality and of life.

THE STORY OF JOB

Job is a biblical character whose faith in God is famously tested by Satan. Being biblical, the story is told from a religious point of view as a story of faith, but we will examine it as a psychological story of self-worth.

Job was the Bill Gates of his time. He was an immensely wealthy man with a large family and huge property holdings. He was devout and fully acknowledged the external source of his well-being, of his successful low self-esteem—that is, God.

At the beginning of the story, God asks Satan his opinion of Job. Satan answers that the only reason Job worships God is because God has given him everything he wants and that the tables would turn if all his blessings were removed.

God gives Satan permission to destroy Job's children and possessions. Job loses everything he holds dear, except his wife. He becomes profoundly depressed. As his troubles mount, his wife encourages him to curse God and give up on life. But in spite of his suffering, Job maintains his faith and does not stop doing what he has always done, which is to worship and praise God. In the end, God rewards Job's faith by doubling his wealth and giving him more children.

Job's route to successful low self-esteem was by pleasing God. He pleased God by believing in Him and was handsomely rewarded in return. The arrangement of successful pleasing leading to successful low self-esteem worked until Satan stepped in. At that point Job's pleasing failed, and instead of reward he received punishment and loss. Successful low self-esteem turned into failed low self-esteem, and without the external supply of worth he became miserable and depressed. Job made no effort to try harder or smarter—he did not switch sides, give up on God and begin to worship other Gods. Nor did he succumb to the use of salves and balms to ease his discomfort. What he did instead was make the decision to accept life on God's (or life's) terms rather than on his, to value life as it was rather than as it was for him. When the chips were down, Job gave up his cognitive narcissism and chose to value life realistically, to value life and himself unconditionally. This restored his self worth and his state of mind.

Job's story exemplifies this transition between a conditional and an unconditional approach to valuing life. When we get what we want, we are satisfied and feel good; when we lose what we value or don't get what we want, we become depressed, no longer value life, and even prefer death. In the face of these terrible losses and narcissistic injuries, we, like Job, can choose life on life's terms. and become our own inalienable source of worth.

In A Nutshell

- When trying harder and smarter or anesthetizing your-self don't help you restore successful low self-esteem, you can give up your reliance on others and instead make an informed decision to become your own source of worth

- Understanding how low self-esteem comes about informs you that **you** are the source of your belief in your own worthlessness, that you based this view on misinformation when you were young and cognitively narcissistic, and that you arrived at this view of yourself out of biological neces-sity, not because you were flawed

- You need to change your view of the world from the narcis-sistic view that says that it is a personal world that is here for you, to either gratify or frustrate you, to a realistic view that says that the world is impersonal and indifferent to you

- Knowing this frees you to choose to value the world realisti-cally and unconditionally on the world's terms, as the world is, warts and all, rather than on your narcissistic and condi-tional terms of how the world is for you

CHAPTER 13

THE IMPLICATIONS OF CHOOSING HEALTHY SELF-ESTEEM

"Freedom's just another word for nothing left to lose."

— *Kris Kristofferson, "Me and Bobby McGee"*

When you choose to be worthwhile, it means that you are now the supplier of your own self-worth. You no longer rely on others or on outside sources for your supply of self-worth; that precious commodity is now yours to provide. You are responsible for your worth.

RESPONSIBILITY

Since you are now responsible for your self-worth, it means that nobody else is responsible for how you feel about yourself. Nobody can make you feel bad, mad, or happy. Only you can. Being responsible

161

for your worth means that you are responsible for your entire self, for all of you, not just your worth.

Just because you take on the responsibility of your self and your worth doesn't mean that the world stops. People continue to do all sorts of things to and around you, and things continue to happen randomly to and around you. Because you are a sentient being, you have an initial emotional reaction to whatever you experience, just as you always did. Your initial emotional responses will continue to span the whole range of emotions right across the board. The difference is that now its up to you to decide what meaning to assign to your experiences. You decide what each situation means to you. You decide how to weigh your emotions and how to respond to the situations that provoke them in the first place. You are now responsible for your emotions and your reactions because you are responsible for yourself—for the self that you are—and for how you are in your life as it unfolds around you. While you do not control what happens to you, you now are able to control the meaning you assign to what happens to you, and in this way, you control your emotions and your reactions. You are no longer a reactor, you determine how you are going to be in a world that is the way it happens to be.

Most people think of themselves as being responsible, and most people are. But there is a difference between being responsible *in* your life and being responsible *for* your life. As I talked about earlier in my own story, before I learned the difference between being responsible in my life and for my life, I considered myself a very responsible person.

Being responsible in your life refers to meeting your obligations, paying your bills, honoring your commitments, and obeying the rules, laws, and conventions of your surroundings. Low self-esteem encourages this kind of responsibility, which is the stuff of social order and coherence. There is nothing unusual or abnormal about this kind of responsibility. It fosters healthy social relations and efficient social function.

Being responsible in your life happens under conditions where others supply you with self-worth and you meet their expectations to receive your share of their approval. Your worth is in the hands of others. As long as others supply you with worth, and as long as you are conditioned by the need to please others, others are responsible for how you are, for how you behave and react, and in that sense, responsible for your life. You are responsible *in* your life, and others are responsible *for* your life.

When others are responsible for your life, they care more about your life than you do, or at least you think they ought to. This is where the expression "I can't live without you" comes from. It is the idea that someone else has to value you more than you do, and that unless someone else values you, your life is not worth having.

But when you are responsible for your worth, you are responsible for everything that is you. This includes your thoughts and feelings, your actions and reactions, your decisions and choices, your changes of heart, and especially your supplies of self-worth—indeed, for your entire being, for your life. You are responsible for how you are with what happens, with how you choose to respond. No one can ever make you angry or crazy again. You can never blame others for how you are or how you feel. People do what they do, and you decide how to be with what you experience of them.

Being responsible for you and your life means that you are not responsible for anyone else. It is not your responsibility to make someone else happy, and you cannot make someone else miserable or depressed. Of course you affect others, just as others affect you, but you do not make them feel or act as they do. How others make meaning of their experience, including their experience of you, is up to them to determine. Others are their responsibility, not yours, just as you are your responsibility, not the responsibility of others.

The only exception to this rule is of course with your children when they are young. You are responsible for them because they are not yet developed enough to be responsible for their own lives. Until they are old enough to be responsible for themselves, you are responsible for them. This is what it means to be a parent: you specifically take on the responsibility for a life other than your own life until such time as that life can take responsibility for themselves.

Being responsible for yourself also means that no one can love you more than you love yourself. Conversely, you cannot love people more than they can themselves. It is only when you are a child that someone loves you more than you can love yourself. This is a useful way to distinguish between adults and children, or at least between the emotional state of adulthood and childhood: an emotional adult is someone who understands that he or she is responsible for him or herself, for loving and valuing themselves more than anyone else can; an emotional child thinks that someone else is responsible for him or her, still expects someone else to care for and love them more than they can themselves.

Thinking along these lines brings Nelson Mandela to mind. As is well known, Mr. Mandela was locked away in prison for twenty-seven years. It was one injustice amid the huge, national injustice that was apartheid. I have never met Mr. Mandela and do not know what he thought about or how he dealt with his situation. I imagine, however, from what has been revealed about his experience of prison life and his conduct after being released, that at some point he made a decision that he and not his jailors would be the one to determine how he would be and behave. His striking lack of bitterness, which wielded a profoundly positive political effect in post-apartheid South Africa, most likely came from his decision to be the one to decide how to think, feel, and react to his tormentors. I imagine that in the privacy of his mind he found a way to be responsible for himself, and for his life, eschewing having others' be responsible for him and his feelings and actions. As the Father of the Nation he found his own way to become an emotional adult and modeled it for his fellow citizens.

THE SHOW IS OVER

Under the old order, where others are responsible for your worth, you perform for positive self-esteem and earn it from others. It is imported from foreign sources, as it were, and paid for by your performance.

When you become the supplier of your own worth, positive self-esteem is no longer the result of your performance. It is, in a sense, the exact opposite: positive self-esteem is a beginning, a starting point, it's where you come from, not where you land up. You do not aspire to self worth, it's your starting point. The outcome of your efforts no longer has any bearing on your worth. Outcomes matter for their own sake, but not for the sake of your worth, they are no longer a determinant of your worth. The way things turn out have practical importance to you, but have no bearing on your self-worth. Your self-esteem is now proclaimed, it is not earned. Once you proclaim your self-worth, you remain worthwhile regardless of the outcome of your efforts, regardless of the result of your actions and performances, regardless of what others think of you and how they respond to you.

So you are freed from the necessity of having to earn your worth, you are free to be and act out of interest and curiosity, not from the obligation to earn esteem.

THE DEVIL WEARS PRADA

The marvelous 2006 film *The Devil Wears Prada* deals with the relationship between achievement and self-worth, and who is responsible for one's self-worth. Andrea (played by Anne Hathaway) is an Ivy League journalism graduate looking to build a prominent career supporting the underdog, but ends up working for a fashion magazine. She seems to have it all: beauty, brains, boyfriend, street smarts, gumption, work ethic—all the ingredients for success. But Miranda (Meryl Streep)—Andrea's tough, emasculating boss—is long on criticism and short on praise.

Andrea does what she knows best: impressing by being clever and competent. And she is extraordinarily accomplished at this, performing near miracles such as getting an advance copy of a new Harry Potter book for Miranda's children before its release. But none of this cuts any ice with the implacable Miranda, who is, to say the least, hard to please. Andrea eats humble pie as a lowly and much put-upon personal assistant who exhorts herself beyond her limits, placing romance, friendship, and ideals in jeopardy in light of her overriding goal of pleasing the unpleasable Miranda.

Eventually Andrea has a meltdown at Miranda's pointed lack of appreciation of her. She complains bitterly to Nigel (Stan Tucci), the art director at the magazine and her informal mentor. In a few brilliant lines, Nigel tells her what she never learned in all her years of college: that just because she thinks she's earned and is entitled to acknowledgement and affirmation, that doesn't mean that she is or that others see her contribution in the same light as she does. The reality is that she is no longer a child, and in the world of emotional adults, as at the magazine, it is not the boss's job to affirm the employees. If Andrea wants to feel affirmed, it is up to her to affirm herself. Her performance is about her performance, not about her worth as a person, and she will suffer if she does not learn how to separate the two.

This is a very difficult lesson for Andrea to learn. As a bright, attractive, energetic young woman she has always performed well and has been well rewarded for her efforts. Her sense of self-worth is inextricably bound up with her performance, her achievements, and the accolades she is accustomed to receiving. She comes face to face with reality beyond the playpen and the college gates. She realizes that nobody owes her anything; her boss has agreed to pay her a salary for her labors, not to supply her with self-esteem. The world will not bow down to her with gratitude for doing what she's contracted to do.

Miranda, representing the real world, doesn't care about what Andrea cares about and is not responsible for Andrea's feelings. Andrea's cares and feelings are Andrea's responsibility, and Andrea needs to learn this if she doesn't want to end up bitter, disappointed, and crushed. Andrea is responsible for her own fulfillment; it is not Miranda's function to fulfill her.

In one sense the film is about Andrea's struggle to learn this lesson. The lesson is beautifully underscored by what happens to Nigel toward the end of the film. Miranda eviscerates him by reneging publicly on a long awaited and much anticipated promise of a hefty promotion. Nigel copes heroically with this humiliating disappointment. He does not throw a tantrum or attack Miranda. He doesn't blame her for hurting his feelings. He swallows hard, owns his pain, and starts to work out his next move. He seems to say, "I am responsible for my ambitions and my dreams, for my choices and my decisions, my commitments and my emotions, and while I cannot control what the world, in this instance Miranda, does and what happens to me, I can control my responses to whatever happens to and around me."

The film says it is childish, silly, and naïve to expect others to take care of you; it is your job to take care of yourself and to allow others to take care of themselves. That is how it is in life, not just in the fast lane of cutthroat fashion journalism, but in the grown-up world of emotional adults. To her credit, Andrea mostly learns this lesson by the time the film ends. Nigel, her mentor, knows it, lives it, and teaches it.

BAD FEELINGS ARE JUST BAD FEELINGS

The world is not a neighborhood narcissistic convenience store. It does not give you what you want just because you're prepared to pay the price. The world is far more unregulated and unpredictable than that. You may be prepared to pay the price, but the world is under no obligation to supply you with what you want. But when you are still stuck in a narcissistic framework, you understand as personal rejection the world's failure to provide you with what you need and are willing to pay for. You think narcissistically that the reason the world does not give you what you are willing to pay for is because you are not good enough to deserve getting what you want, so the world deliberately withholds from you. This is the same script you had when you were a three-year-old and your mother was not there when you needed her. Not getting what you need is a reflection of your inherent lack of worth, and being unworthy feels bad.

Emotions are your sixth sense. When something disappointing happens, you are supposed to feel bad, just as when things happen in line with your preferences, you are supposed to feel good. It is no different from when you hear a noise or see something; your senses draw your attention to the stimulus. Your emotions function in the same way. Something happens that is or isn't to your liking, and you have an emotional reaction to that event. So you are supposed to feel good under certain circumstances and bad under others. This is how you are constructed as a sentient human being. Life as we know it without emotions would not be possible.

There is nothing unusual, wrong, or pathological about feeling bad. We all feel bad at times—and ought to. The nature of feelings is that they pass; they shift as the circumstances around us shift. This is no different from any other sense we experience: what is noise one moment stops being noise when we close the door or change the channel. Emotions change as circumstances change.

One of the conditions our emotions respond to is our thoughts—specifically, our thoughts of ourselves. Negative thoughts provoke negative emotions. Thinking you are worthless feels bad, just as you'd expect. When your thoughts about your worth are tied to results, to outcomes, to what others might think of you, as it does with emotional narcissism, you feel bad when the results are not to your liking, because you didn't get your way. Moreover, you end up feeling worse because you interpret failure as meaning that you are not worthwhile. You now feel bad for two reasons: first because you didn't get what you wanted and second because not getting what you wanted means you're not good enough. Not being good enough makes it less likely that you will get what you want in the future. In this way you are stuck in a vicious cycle of feeling bad.

But when you become the source of your own worth, when your worth is no longer dependent on outcomes, you still feel bad when things don't turn out the way you prefer, but you do not compound your bad feelings by making them mean something negative about you. You no longer get caught up in the vicious cycle of making your bad feelings worse. Disappointment remains mere disappointment, not personal inadequacy that can spiral into depression.

Depression as an illness may still occur. There is always the potential for the machinery that regulates mood to break down. But when you remove the powerful negative force of failed low self-esteem by transforming yourself into someone who is responsible for your worth, the chances of your mood-regulating machinery breaking down is greatly reduced.

Once you have chosen to be worthwhile, even when bad things happen to and around you—which will continue to happen because that's life, even when you feel unhappy, disappointed, bereft, rejected, frustrated, or angry—you are still worthy. Your bad feelings do not determine your self-worth. You do. Your bad feelings are just bad feelings; they are not a measure of your worth, and they have nothing to do with your value as a person. Your bad feelings will pass, but your esteem is constant. You feel bad because something happens where feeling bad is the appropriate way to feel, and your feelings are congruent with your experience. But feeling bad does not mean that you are bad. Your worth has been decided by an informed decision, and feelings cannot alter that.

EMOTIONAL FREEDOM

As we have seen, narcissism is not only natural but is important and vitally necessary for social function. Once it becomes a burden, however, you have the capacity to get beyond it, to become an emotional adult rather than stay stuck in the state of failed low self-esteem, which is rooted in narcissism. You can free yourself from this state in the ways to be outlined in the next chapter. You can free yourself from much of what is called depression. You can free your emotions to respond to actual reality and not to distorted narcissistic misinterpretations of reality. You can be free to be as you wish, to be as you choose to be, rather than be how you think others want you to be. This is emotional freedom.

Emotional freedom is not the same as personal freedom and is not dependent on it. Emotional freedom is obviously not the same as economic or political freedom, and is not dependent on either. You can be politically, economically and personally free, but remain an emotional slave to the wills of others. Just think of any one of a number of celebrities or anyone else who seems to wield great personal and economic freedom, and consider their enslavement to publicity and/or drugs, and you will see how emotional freedom is different from all these other and more familiar forms of freedom.

The concept of emotional freedom is interesting in that you can think about the word *free* as both an adjective and a verb. When you take on emotional responsibility, and enter the state of emotional adulthood, you become free. You become free from the obligation to please others and free to choose how you want to be. You make these emotional changes and become free, entering into a state of freedom.

The notion of free will is usually understood as a quality but in choosing emotional adulthood, you are in fact freeing your will. Perhaps the idea that we are created with free will means just that: that we are created with the intrinsic capacity to free our wills, to free them from enslavement to other wills, to free them from the compulsion to please other people. Instead of living our lives vicariously through the will of others, we have the capacity to free our wills and live by our own volition instead. Perhaps this is the fulfillment of our highest strivings and our deepest destiny: to reach emotional adulthood, the place where we can transcend the necessity of living vicariously through the will of others to live out our own desires freely come by.

It should be noted that you cannot short-circuit this process of becoming an emotional adult and living with this type and level of freedom. You cannot reach this point without first passing through the earlier phases of binding your will to the necessity to please others and learning how to comply with the norms and rules of your community. The challenge is learning how to get beyond this earlier stage.

If you imagine this early stage as equivalent to submitting your will to the will of others or to the will of the common good, you can think of your life as something you rent from the community, from others. Freeing your will is a process whereby you become the owner of your life. You are no longer a renter but a proud owner. The capacity to become free, to be able to free your will, to become the owner of your life is latent within you. It is part of the human condition to strive to reach for this freedom and to achieve it.

Once achieved, this freedom cannot be taken from you. It is not dependent on or determined by anyone else. It exists only between you and yourself. It is inalienable. Life circumstances, laws, and social norms place all kinds of restrictions on your degrees of freedom to act, but they can never place restrictions on your freedom to be the way you choose to be in any given situation.

As someone who chooses self-worth, you are free to make whatever decisions you wish about how to expend your energies and resources, within the confines of what is possible under your circumstances. You may make the exact same choices as you did as an emotionally unfree person, and, to an outsider, you and your life may look identical to how they looked before. What matters is your experience of your choices. Even though you do the same things and make the same choices, your experience of them will be completely different—free of resentment, rancor, or depression.

SELFISHNESS AND SELF-RELIANCE

It may appear as though the case I make for breaking the bonds of narcissism and becoming self-determining encourages selfishness.

After all, I urge you to give up being determined by others, and to stop considering others' opinions when deciding how to be in your life. You may construe this as making a case for becoming indifferent to the feelings and interests of others, for becoming heartless. You may understand becoming emotionally free as freeing yourself to exploit and take advantage of others, because you no longer care what they think of you. It is time, then, to explore the differences between selfishness and self-reliance.

Being emotionally self-reliant, to have transcended the limitations of narcissism and taken responsibility for your worth and your life means specifically that you do not rely on anyone else for your worth. Therefore, no one else has anything you need in order for you to be worthwhile. Everything you need is within you. You are self-sufficient. So you don't need anything from anyone else to be okay and have no interest in depriving anyone of what belongs to them. If selfish is taking something that belongs to someone else for you, then you have no need to be selfish.

This doesn't mean that you can't compete with others. You may share a similar interest in acquiring the same thing as someone else, and you may compete for it, and compete vigorously. But your well-being and sense of worth are not affected or determined by the outcome of that competition. You can afford to lose, because losing does not make you a loser; it just means that your will did not prevail. You remain every bit as worthwhile as you were before the competition, because your worth is independent of any performance or outcome.

Also, your appreciation of your own innate worth necessarily sensitizes you to the innate worth of other people. Since your worth is not dependent on anything, and is not a result or an outcome, you recognize that other peoples' worth is also not the result of their performance. They have the same intrinsic worth as you do, and for the same reason – if life is worth having unconditionally, your life is

worth having unconditionally, and so is all life worth having unconditionally, so all people are inherently worthwhile just as you are. You
naturally treat precious things well. Since everyone else is every bit as
valuable as you are, you have no incentive to treat others as precious
and valuable, so you have no incentive to behave selfishly towards
others, no incentive to harm others just as you have no incentive to
harm yourself.

There is now a double set of reasons for valuing and not exploit-
ing others: you recognize that others are as valuable as you are, and
they have nothing you need for you to be okay with yourself. As you
disentangle your interests from your worth, you are able to respond
to others based on a rational appreciation of their inherent worth
that removes the need for selfishness.

Becoming responsible for your worth, choosing to be worthwhile, is about self-reliance, not selfishness. You become reliant on
yourself for your worth, and for your life. This happens in a way that
obviates selfishness.

CHAPTER 14

BECOMING THE CHANGE

"To think is easy. To act is difficult. To act as one thinks is the most difficult of all."

— *Goethe*

MAKING YOUR DECISION LIVE

Change is a two-step procedure. First you commit to change, and then you become the change.

To commit to change, you must learn what you need to know in order to make the decision to be different, and then you make that decision based on what you have learned. This is the informed decision-making or the commitment part. It is much harder to change without information because knowledge is power, and information powers the change you choose. Without information, you have little power to change or to sustain your commitment to change.

Having made the decision to change, you have to apply what you have learned and become what you have decided to become. To possess the knowledge but not apply it is sterile or academic; you just become someone who knows what you know. You are not different just by virtue of knowing about how to be different. You may spend hours in the library learning everything you need to know about being a ballet dancer, and may then decide to become a ballet dancer. At that point, all you are is someone who has decided to be a ballet dancer. You are not a ballet dancer until you start to do the things that ballet dancers do, until you start applying what you have learned to your actions and your life.

It is the same when you decide to be worthwhile. Until you put what you have decided into effect, you are just someone who has decided to become worthwhile, but not yet someone who is worthwhile. To become worthwhile, you must give up being how you were, which is having your worth determined by others, and start to determine your own worth. Your old familiar way of being can be understood as a habit, a particular habit of thought. And so you can think of this as changing a habit, the thought habit of having others determine your worth, and cultivating the new habit of determining your own worth.

There are different approaches to changing habits. I will suggest a generic approach to changing this thought habit, an approach that can be broken down into three distinct steps that can be considered the three Rs of emotional literacy.

THE THREE R'S OF EMOTIONAL LITERACY

Step 1. RECOGNIZE

The first step in applying your decision to be responsible for your own self-worth is to recognize the moments in your daily life when you find yourself thinking about your lack of worth—your need to please someone else or not to offend someone, for fear of incurring their displeasure and forfeiting their positive regard for you. This scenario is an indication that someone else determines your worth, not you, and so is an example of the workings of the old habit of your worth being determined by others. Situations that reflect the workings of this habit crop up frequently for most people, so you should not be at a loss for situations where you can recognize the old pattern or habit.

In this first step, the only thing required is that you recognize the habit.

This shouldn't be difficult because even if you don't immediately recognize the habit by observing your thoughts in the moment, your emotions will help you out. Your emotions, being a sixth sense, an alerting mechanism that directs your attention to potential threats, will draw your attention to situations where you feel uneasy at the prospect of displeasing and being judged negatively by someone. So your feelings will make you aware of the old habit, and this is what you need to recognize as step 1 in the process.

You do not have to do anything when you recognize the old habit. It is sufficient just to recognize it and get used to recognizing it when it makes it's presence felt. It does not matter if you miss it on occasion, because life will keep exposing you to situations that provoke the old pattern and the negative feelings that accompany it. So during this first step, pay attention to your feelings and observations, and train yourself to recognize the situations that evoke the old pattern of needing to please and appease others because others determine your worth.

There is no need to feel disappointed when the old habit asserts itself. It is unrealistic to expect that it will disappear just because you decided to replace it. Recognizing it is like accepting an invitation to do something, in this case, something different. Without the invitation, you cannot participate; without recognizing the habit, you cannot begin to change it.

Step 2. REMEMBER

Having recognized the old habit, the next step is simply to remember that you decided to change the habit. That's all. Just remember that you made a thoughtful and informed decision to be different, to be the source of your own worth. I have worked with more than one person who returned to a session saying they remembered the first step, *recognize*, but forgot this second one, the step of remembering.

After recognizing the old pattern, you need to remember that you decided to be worthwhile, that your worth is now set by you and not by anyone else. Since you are most likely to recognize the old pattern in moments of discomfort, you have to train yourself to remember that you decided to be different at these awkward times.

Step 3. REHEARSE

Having recognized the old habit and reminded yourself that you decided to be different, you next have to be different, or to behave differently. But the problem is that you do not know how to be or behave differently. How could you when you have no experience of being different? So what do you do?

Well, you need to think about it.

Since you have none of your own experience to draw on, you have to engage your imagination and think about other people's experience. You need to imagine how someone else might deal with the situation, especially someone else who you think has the capacity you're trying to develop. What would the Dalai Lama do? What would Nelson Mandela do? What would Mother Theresa do? What would Jesus do?

It is not realistic to expect the perfect answer to spring to mind right away. You need to take and make the time to consider different possibilities. In the beginning you will need to leave the situation without a suitable way to respond. Your best response might be to check your habitual response without having an alternative. But you walk away and think about someone you think has healthy self-esteem, someone who is self-reliant for their worth, and how they may handle the situation.

You may think about someone you know, or know about. You may think about someone living or dead, real or fictional. You think about how a character from a movie or a book responded in similar situations. It is an exercise in imagination and so you engage your imagination to think about it.

The wonderful thing about your mind is not just that it can think and imagine, but that it is private. You can think whatever you like in the privacy of your mind, and no one is any the wiser. This gives you enormous freedom to think about all sorts of things, especially about how your responses might look if you were reacting as someone responsible for your worth.

You take as much time as you want thinking about this. You think about different ways of being. It's like an actor who is rehearsing in front of a mirror. You try different ways and repeat them over and over to test if they feel right, if they work. You refine them in the privacy of your mind and prepare yourself for the next time a similar situation arises.

Like the actor who rehearses and rehearses and rehearses, and finally leaves the dressing room and appears on stage, so it is with you. You rehearse and practice and rehearse and practice. Eventually you leave the practice room and are ready to try it out. The next time a situation presents itself, you give it a shot. And you see what happens.

What you find is that when things work out, when your new way of being works and doesn't backfire, that there's no catastrophic or traumatic response from the other person, you may repeat the new way of dealing with those kinds of situations. Things you try that don't work you discard and try something else.

Over time these new ways of thinking and reacting replace your old habitual ways and become your new way of being. This is how you replace the old habits and cultivate new ones.

It is obvious that this is easier said than done, that it is hard. Habits by their nature resist change, so changing a habit, especially a thought habit that's been part of you from before you can remember, takes effort. It is by far the hardest part, and much harder than the previous steps of learning, understanding, deciding, recognizing and remembering. This is the hardest part, this is where the real work of change happens.

It does not take courage to do something that is familiar and when you can anticipate the outcome. When you try something new and cannot anticipate the outcome and don't know whether you'll be safe or not, you need to be brave. So trying something new, this integral step in changing yourself, requires a lot of thought, preparation and ultimately courage. But there is no escaping this crucial step. This is the final step on the road to change, to being different, to being the person responsible for yourself and for your worth.

THE COURAGE TO CHANGE: WHAT WOULD PETER DO?

There is an incident in the story of Peter Pan that highlights this principle of using your imagination to think about how a self-reliant person would handle a situation before you have learned how.

Peter Pan is an orphan who lives on the island of Neverland. He recruits other orphans from the streets of London and brings them to live in Neverland. They are the Lost Boys and he is the captain of the Lost Boys. Peter brings Wendy to the island to be a mother to the Lost Boys. Also living on the island is Captain Hook and the pirates, who happen to be orphans as well, the Red Indians and the Wild Beasts. Island life consists of the Lost Boys being chased by the Pirates, who in turn are chased by the Red Indians, who in their turn are chased by the Wild Beasts.

One day Peter is away and things suddenly change on the island. The Wild Beasts chase the lost Boys, not the Red Indians.

One of the Lost Boys, Nibs, is cornered by a pack of wolves. He appeals to the other Lost Boys for help, and the boys make the decision to help him. This is a decision to change from being the protected to becoming protectors. But with Peter away, the boys don't know how to help him, or how to change. "But what can we do, what can we do?" they ask. And then, in unison, they ask themselves the question, "What would Peter do?" In the next breath, time being very short, they pronounce what they think Peter would do: he would turn his back on the wolves, bend over, look at them upside down from between his legs, and walk slowly towards them. So they try it. Luckily, it works, and the wolves take off in fright. Nibs is saved, and the Lost Boys change from being rescued to rescuers.

Considering what the Boys did, it seems very foolish. Turning your back on a bunch of snarling predators is suicidal. But, however daft that was, you'll agree that it was different. If you decide to change, to become different, then you must be different, you must do things differently. Which is precisely what the Boys did. Their courage is also easy to recognize – they were very courageous putting themselves in such a vulnerable position to the wolves.

DELIA TAKES ON AUTHORITY

Delia, like so many people I have worked with, was stuck in the old arrangement whereby others determined her self-worth. She was always at pains not to offend people, in case they turned against her. She was non-confrontational to the point where she would not assert herself. During our work together, she realized that sooner or later she would have to face her fears of disapproval and rejection and speak her mind, even in situations where she suspected that her opinion might not be welcome.

Eventually a situation arose where she had the opportunity to speak her mind. Her neighbor had called the police after her boyfriend threatened to assault her. The neighbor was upset and not terribly coherent as she provided the police officer with her account of what had happened. Delia, who had come over to give her neighbor support, saw that the police officer was getting irritated at her answers to his questions and felt that he was speaking disrespectfully to her. The moment had come. Delia knew she had to speak her mind. She was afraid, fearing that if she spoke her mind, he would think she was "a stupid bitch" and might turn on her. Despite her fear, she screwed up her courage and politely told the officer what she thought, which was that he was being unprofessional. This was her personal nightmare, that she offend someone and provoke their ire and rejection. The officer was rude and dismissive of her, just as she had feared, but he did not turn on her, and Delia's world did not come crashing down.

Delia was proud of what she had done. She appreciated that it was a huge and significant step for her. She had spoken her mind, had drawn someone's disapproval, and had survived. The incident became a touchstone that allowed her to try out different ways of responding in other situations where she would previously have remained silent and resented herself for it. Delia practiced being different, being responsible for her own self-worth, and became more and more comfortable in her new role.

THE CHANGE THAT CHANGED MARGO

Then there was Margo, who had always swallowed any criticism toward anyone in case it led to disapproval and rejection. She was entirely unable to assert herself, and the very thought of doing so made her intensely anxious. Her personality was defined by her doormat and martyr-like behaviors.

One day, toward the end of her therapy, she was paying for something in a store and noticed the clerk had given her the wrong change. She screwed up her courage and pointed this out to him, something she had never dared to do before. In her mind she anticipated an ugly and humiliating scene, but the clerk simply checked the change he had given her, apologized for his error, and gave her the correct amount. She drew enormous courage from this and launched herself into a new mode of assertiveness based on a growing conviction of her inherent worth, reinforced by further experiences of asserting herself and dealing with any consequences. She became the person she wanted to be: self-reliant and not afraid of what others might think of her.

In A Nutshell

- The 3 R formula for implementing change:
    - o Recognize – the old pattern of having your worth determined by others
    - o Remember – that you decided to determine your own worth
    - o Rehearse – how someone responsible for their own worth might behave in the particular situation you're in
- Then Repeat the ways of being that work

CHAPTER 15

CHANNELING JENNY

Throughout these pages, I have outlined a way of understanding the pervasiveness of low self-esteem and its role in generating human misery. I have suggested a new way to think about its origins and role in our lives—and to think of it not as a sign of failure, but rather as a necessary element of healthy social development. The fact that it can go sour does not invalidate its initial purpose and value. The point is that we have the latent ability to transcend the low self-esteem state and to become suppliers of our own worth.

In order to tap into this latent potential to become responsible for supplying our own worth, we need to understand the origins and the purpose of our self-esteem. We are unlikely to do this unless we experience some malfunction to our self-esteem and emotional systems. If provoked to do so, we can learn to transcend the limitations and downsides of low self-esteem and learn to acquire healthy self-esteem by becoming our own source of self-worth and giving up our reliance on others.

While difficult and requiring effort, it is entirely possible to achieve. Through my personal and professional experience I have witnessed profound personal changes in people willing to meet this challenge.

When Jenny came in for her sixth and final session, she looked bright and cheerful and said how much better she felt, that she had "got it". She said that she understood how to stop making things that happened to her mean something about her and her worth or lack of worth and, because of this, that she was able to be her own source of worth. She told me that her husband was an alcoholic and that when he drank, which was every night, it was she and not him who would feel sick to her stomach and it was she, not him, who would wake up the next morning with the hangover. She told me that she thought her husband drank because of her, that he drank because she was not good enough for him, and that if she were good enough for him, he would not drink. His drinking made her sick, literally physically and emotionally, because she misinterpreted his drinking to be about her when, of course, it wasn't. She came to understand that his drinking, even though it affected her, had nothing to do with her, and that it was about him and him alone. Once she stopped personalizing his behavior and making his actions mean something about her, she freed herself from the downward spiral of devaluing herself and started to feel very well, very energized and better than she could ever remember feeling in her life. She felt sad for her husband and his destructive drinking but no longer bad about herself.

We can all be like Jenny.

CHAPTER 16

IN A NUTSHELL

- Low self-esteem comes about around age three as part of normal healthy development

- At that young age when there are times that your needs are not met, you mistakenly understand that you are not worth being cared for

- It is part of the normal and healthy experience of separation that there are times when your mother simply isn't there when you need her and so your needs go unmet

- It is part of normal healthy cognitive development to think that whatever happens to you is about you, so your mother's absence is about you, not her

- This leads you to the mistaken belief that because your mother is not there to care for you, and that you do not receive care, that you are not worth being cared for

- This is the Humpty Dumpty experience of abandonment, that together with your natural cognitive narcissism, leads you to the conviction that you are inherently worthless

- This conviction of your inherent worthlessness motivates you to try to please your mother to make sure she cares for you (and ensures your survival)

- You mistakenly believe that it is your efforts to please that make your mother care for you. You conclude from successfully pleasing your mother that you are worthwhile, and that's how you come to experience successful low self-esteem

- Successfully pleasing others is how you get to feel worthwhile and experience high self-esteem, or what can be more accurately termed successful low self-esteem

- When your ability to make others value you fails, usually through loss or change, you regress to experiencing yourself as worthless

- Faced with this regression to worthlessness, you try harder or smarter to make others value you

- If and when that doesn't work, and you are stuck not knowing how to make others value you, you are likely to suppress the negative feelings of being worthless with drugs or pills

- There is another way to deal with failed low self-esteem, which is by making the informed decisions to become your own source of worth instead of relying on others to provide you with your sense of worth

- An informed decision requires both specific information and a specific decision, all of which are outlined in chapter 12

- Having made the decision to be your own source of worth, and to be worthwhile, you need to practice putting that outlook into effect. This involves changing the habitual way you think of yourself and your worth. This can be accomplished by using a 3 step procedure (the 3 Rs of Emotional Literacy) to change, firstly Recognizing the presence of the old habitual way of thinking of your worth, then Remembering that you decided to change it, and thirdly Rehearsing different ways of thinking of yourself and behaving in specific situations. Chapter 13 provides a framework for putting your decision into practice and making it a living part of you.

Made in the USA
Charleston, SC
12 May 2013